P9-CRH-373

PREACHING IN A SCIENTIFIC AGE

PREACHING IN A SCIENTIFIC AGE

BY

A. C. CRAIG

Lecturer in Biblical Studies, Glasgow University

THE WARRACK LECTURES FOR 1953

CHARLES SCRIBNER'S SONS
NEW YORK

Contents

I

The Dilemma of the Preacher

A YEAR or so after I was ordained to the ministry, I happened one day to meet Principal Alexander Martin on Princes Street in Edinburgh, and he greeted me with the question, 'Well, how's the preaching going?' When I replied that I was finding it very difficult, he exclaimed, 'Preaching's not difficult, man: it's impossible!'

The epigram struck me forcibly, spoken as it was before Reinhold Niebuhr had accustomed a generation of theogical students to speak with easy familiarity about 'impossible possibilities', as though these were homely creatures like puppies or potatoes. Yet it was intended, I have little doubt, not as a metaphysical aphorism, but rather as a bracing practical hint to a callow preacher. If in one of his seminars one summoned up courage to make an observation, Dr. Martin had a very disconcerting way of saying, 'Yes . . . yes . . . but will you please amplify a little?' It is a matter of lasting regret to me that I did not think of using these very words in reply to him that day when he said, 'Preaching's not difficult: it's impossible!' Not that it would have disconcerted him: it takes more than that to disconcert a theological professor, let alone a Principal; but it might have elicited a notable amplification. He might have cleared his throat in a way he had of doing when he intended not so much to speak as to utter, and said something to this effect: 'Young man, do not imagine that you will ever master the glamorous, elusive art of preaching. If you have the authentic call to it, it will enslave you, enchant you, tease you, confound you all your days; and in the end you will still have to say, "I have not attained, I only press toward the mark of this high calling." If you ever begin to feel that you have mastered the art, if you find that your sermons begin to write themselves between a reading of the morning paper and lunch-time, then beware: it will almost certainly mean, not that you have mastered the art of preaching, but that one of the myriad forms of egotism has mastered you. The Christian pulpit, even if only regarded as a stance of utterance in a horizontal plane of reality, is always ringed about by perplexities, some perennial and inherent in the nature of preaching, others adventitious and special to a given era, others again springing from the individuality of the preacher, down to the state of his liver. Do not imagine that you will ever wholly overcome even these horizontal problems and difficulties. Resign yourself to a lifelong state of dilemma in respect of even these, at best to a partial and painful measure of extrication, like that of a man struggling through a thicket of briars who before he wins free from one tangle of thorns is clutched by another. And a greater dilemma remains: the Christian pulpit stands not only in a mundane dimension of reality but also in the supernatural plane of faith, and the man who speaks from it is charged to speak not only about God but from God, not only as reporter but also as ambassador. In the seemly Anglican usage the preacher, before he gives out his text, utters the words, "In the name of the Father, and of the Son, and of the Holy Ghost."

This august formula sets the occasion in its true perspective. Duly heard, it reminds the listener that his ear ought to be tuned to catch not merely a man's words but through them God's Word. Duly spoken, it expresses on the part of the preacher at the very least a sense of grave responsibility and even, as Barth suggests in one of his earliest books, "a fundamental alarm". To the end of time preaching can only be an embarrassed stammering. Do not call it difficult, therefore: call it impossible, and then go on with it humbly, trusting in Him with whom "all things are possible".'

In some such vein Principal Martin might conceivably have amplified his epigram, without meaning, however, that the attempt should not be made by every possible means to ease the difficulties and solve the problems attendant on the preacher's office. In these lectures I propose to consider mainly certain of those problems which I have called adventitious and special to a given era, but it may be worth while at the outset to remind ourselves of problems inherent in preaching as such. In doing so, it will be prudent in the time at our disposal to limit consideration to the typical kind and occasion of preaching, namely, preaching to an ordinary congregation. Preaching to a specialized kind of audience, whatever may be its principle of segregation—whether on the score of age or educational status or particular function and interest—is a different and on the whole an easier matter in which some difficulties are automatically eased, although it has its own special problems. The most exacting occasion is preaching at the regular diet of the Church's worship to which the invitation is as wide as humanity itself.

A starting-point, convenient in that it provides a scheme of classification, is afforded by the old educational tag that the verb *docere* governs two accusatives. Woe to the man who sets up to be a teacher and forgets that his business is to teach John Latin, who counts himself sufficiently equipped for his task if he knows all about the queer habits of *quin* and next to nothing about the vagaries of poor little John! The chief advances in modern pædagogy are due at bottom to the discovery of John—his limitations as an individual, his rights as a potential person, his destiny as a human being. Woe also, by the same token, to the teacher who may understand John well enough but not *quin*, not his subject! In neither case can there be teaching.

May the maxim about the two accusatives be transferred without qualification to the realm of preaching? Formal grammar answers no: *prædicare* governs one accusative only. Thus also might answer the kind of minister, not always conspicuously successful in his profession, often more pontifical than persuasive, who loves to quote the text from Ezekiel, 'thou shalt speak my words unto them, whether they will hear or whether they will forbear', and who twice a Sunday barks resoundingly in his pulpit like an angry watchdog in a kennel. Thus also must have thought the incumbent who is said to have conducted a service in a completely empty church on a wintry morning, preaching his prepared sermon to the last word and justifying the expense of energy on the ground that he must be faithful to all the duties of his office. Well, to conduct worship in an empty church may make sublime sense where the officiant consciously represents in that place the whole company of the faithful and conscientiously undertakes the high task of intercession for the world, but surely to preach in an empty church would only make nonsense, tinged perhaps with a kind of quixotic heroism. At any rate I take for granted that preaching resembles teaching, and encounters like difficulties, being an art of communication, an effort to mediate between an *x* and a *y* made by a *z*. The *x* in preaching is the Gospel, the Word of God; the *y* is mankind, called by the Gospel to be the worshipping family of God; and the *z* is an individual man commissioned to be the channel between these two.

So far it is plain sailing. The problems start up whenever a substantive and detailed exposition of the symbols is demanded. What is the Word of God? In what sense is it to be related to the Bible, to nature, to history, to the sciences and philosophies of men? How is it related to theology? Can our scholars and professors catch the Word in a net of doctrine and hand it over to the preacher authentic and whole and alive? Or is the Chinese proverb true which says that doctrine can catch truth, as a fisherman catches a fish, but truth dies in its net?

And supposing you think you know well enough what is the Word, the Church's Latin, and how it is to be related to the Bible and all the rest, who in their inmost being are these people whom you face across the massive gilt-edged volume on the pulpit-desk? On a good morning there may be three or four hundred of them in a solid array which somehow gives them the appearance of an understandable and manageable single entity. Or there may be only a score or two in knots and dots among the pews, a thin and wintry scattering which may a little chill the preacher's spirit but which serves to bring out his proper problem as a preacher, namely, that he is addressing persons, each of them a world, each of them a citadel of privacy complete with moat and portcullis, tapestried chambers, dungeons and ghosts of the past. What do you know about these mysterious buildings behind the window-slits of each of which—some lit up, some dull and blank, some perhaps curtained in slumber as the discourse proceeds—a life goes on as private and particular and complex as your own? Is the language you propose to use the mother-tongue of their tenants, so that you can reckon on being understood? Or are you like the colonel who saw no reason why any foreigner should not understand English if he spoke it loud enough? Or like the Cambridge professor who began a sermon to college servants with the words, 'The ontological argument for the existence of the Deity has of late years, I grant you, mainly owing to the onslaughts of a destructive and largely Teutonic criticism, been relegated to a subordinate place in the armoury of the Christian apologetic'? And if you command the intelligible idiom, can you use it with such sympathetic understanding of your hearers' inner lives that it will convey the Word past ignorance and prejudice, suspicion and fear, and lodge it in their heart and conscience? All these are daunting questions, and they have taken no account of the prosaic but important respect already alluded to in which the preacher's task must always be more perplexing than the teacher's. It is difficult enough to pitch the teaching of a graded class, whose members are of like age and have been exposed to the same previous disciplines, at a level fair at once to the dullard and the dux. The difficulty is aggravated where, as in preaching, the audience comprises people of all ages and classes, and all degrees of mental and spiritual attainment. How are you to pitch your utterance for such heterogeneous hearing?

And supposing all these problems to be solved in one measure or another, the thorniest problem of all still remains: who are you yourself who venture to stand in a pulpit? The passage from Barth in which he speaks of 'a fundamental alarm' is well worth quoting in full in this reference:[1]

> 'Do the prophets and apostles, not to speak of Jesus Christ, give us the impression of being people who have succeeded, who could at the end look back upon a blessed and satisfying life? Strange that we do so much better than they! What can it mean? It means above all that we should feel a fundamental alarm. What are you doing, you man, with the Word of *God* upon *your* lips? Upon what grounds do you assume the rôle of mediator between heaven and earth? Who has authorized you to take your place there and to generate religious feeling? And, to crown all, to do so with results, with success? Did one ever hear of such overweening presumption, such Titanism, or—to speak less classically but more clearly—such brazenness? One does not with impunity cross the boundaries of mortality! One does not with impunity usurp the prerogatives of God! But does not the profession of the ministry inevitably involve both? *Is* not the whole situation in the Church an illustration of man's chronic presumption, which is really worse here than in any other field? Can a minister be saved? I

[1] *The Word of God and the Word of Man* (Hodder and Stoughton), p. 125.

would answer that with men this is impossible; but with God all things *are* possible. *God* may pluck us as a brand out of the fire. But so far as *we* know, there is no one who deserves the wrath of God more abundantly than the ministers. We may as well acknowledge that *we* are under judgment—and I mean judgment not in any spiritual, religious, or otherwise innocuous sense but in the utmost realism! Moses and Isaiah, Jeremiah and Jonah knew of a certainty why they did *not* want to enter into the preacher's situation. . . . Who dares, who can, preach, knowing what preaching is?'

Translating into a milder idiom this outburst, the intensity of which spatters the page with italics as though gusts of emotion had every now and then blown the type sideways, one might say: preach if you dare, but remember that you preach at your soul's peril. That being so, you had better seriously ask who you are before you begin, and by what title you venture to open your lips.

Up to this point I have done nothing except pose problems, but there is plenty of evidence that these are not entirely insoluble. There was a time in Scotland, the last lingering phase of which I am old enough to remember, when they embarrassed nobody seriously, for to them all, at the time of the Reformation, there had been worked out solutions so profound, so coherent, and so commanding for the thought of those days that they gradually came to entrench themselves as secular presuppositions in the general mind. Presuppositions are to life what foundations are to a building, the sub-structure you don't worry about until cracks appear in the walls; or what eyes are to readers, the organs they never look at but see by. Basic to the massive Reformation scheme was the place it gave to the Bible, and nothing in the *Westminster Confession* is more remarkable than what it says in this regard. Let me remind you of two key-sentences from its first chapter:

> 'The authority of the holy scripture, for which it ought to be believed and obeyed, dependeth not upon the testimony of any man or church, but wholly upon God (who is truth itself), the author thereof; and therefore it is to be received, because it is the Word of God.'
>
> 'The Old Testament in Hebrew (which was the native language of the people of God of old), and the New Testament in Greek (which at the time of the writing of it was most generally known to the nations), being immediately inspired by God, and by his singular care and providence kept pure in all ages, are therefore authentical; so as in all controversies of religion, the Church is finally to appeal unto them.'

Consistently with these affirmations, Scripture is cited as authority for every sentence of the *Confession* itself, the references to chapter and verse running along the foot of the pages like a sustained pedal-note above which intricate harmonies are built.

Now, where it is a case of dealing with ordinary men and women, who like to have things plain and pat, such a position has the supreme advantage of being lucid, crisp and unequivocal, so that it even admits of pictorial enforcement. I remember well an illustrated New Testament, a thin folio volume in marbled covers, over which as a small boy I used to pore on Sunday afternoons, not without awe and trembling of spirit, for some of the engravings at the book of Revelation were fearsome. Down the sides of one page angels of judgment were diving, whose glittering lances were well and truly aimed at the sinners cowering and writhing at the foot of it. What a mercy it was, I used to think, that those dreadful angels, paralysed in print, could never, never, never dive to the bottom of that terrible page! I liked best the head-pieces to the Gospels, pictures of old men of gentle and tranquil countenance who wrote with great quill-pens to the whispered dictation of fluttering angels. Even a small boy could grasp the theory thus depicted, the theory of God's Word having been inerrantly reduced to writing through the agency of men telephonically inspired from heaven. What a child could grasp in the last decade of the nineteenth century the ordinary men and women of our land had lived by for centuries back, and it had given them what all men need for sturdy walking on the earth, the assurance of firm ground beneath their feet. But they had not only accepted the formal authority of the Bible; they had also absorbed its substance, and that both by personal study of its text and in the manner congenial to the temper of mind forged in the fires of the Reformation, namely, in terms of the doctrinal system which the Reformers had drawn from Scripture and embodied in confession and catechism. You probably all know the story of a great gathering of children once addressed in our church's Assembly Hall by D. L. Moody. In the course of his address he happened to ask the rhetorical question, 'What is prayer?' and was somewhat taken aback when hundreds of hands shot up. 'Very well,' he said, 'answer the question.' Whereupon a chorus of young voices recited the noble words of the Shorter Catechism:

> 'Prayer is an offering up of our desires unto God, for things agreeable to his will, in the name of Christ, with confession of our sins, and thankful acknowledgment of his mercies.'

Let the incident stand as symbol of the penetration of Scotland's soul by the work of the Reformers, a process never complete—granite being granite, and whisky threepence a gill—yet penetrative enough to give the nation a homogeneous character which could fairly be called Christian. Moreover—and this is the immediately relevant point—it was a process in the course of which all the questions posed at the beginning of this lecture found workable answers which everyone came to understand and accept.

The Word of God was the Bible, and the Bible was the Word of God. Of course, the *Westminster Confession* complicates this flat equation by introducing on either side of it a vibrant factor in the conception of the Spirit who inspired the writers of the Bible and who witnesses to its truth in the hearts of the elect. But this important elaboration of the doctrine, which supplies it as it were with a nervous system and ought to preclude anything like bibliolatry, would seem never to have counted so much with ordinary people as did the idea of an objective revelation, the materialization of the Word of God in a book. With the Bible in his hand and its essential truths displayed for him in skeletonic form in confession and catechism, every bone of which was either 'expressly set down in scripture, or by good and necessary consequence deduced from scripture', the ordinary man felt he could know all he needed to know concerning the pilgrim life of earth and the states of bliss and woe beyond.

Within the framework of this grand persuasion, the other questions answered themselves. Remember here, by the way, this significant aspect of the old days, that for many years and over large areas of our land the Church was not only the unquestioned religious authority but also practically the sole cultural agency. It had no serious rival, with the important exception of the devil, in fashioning the people's outlook, furnishing their minds and influencing their habits of life. In these circumstances, and thus brought up from earliest youth on Bible and Catechism, a congregation well understood exactly what it was, and so did its minister. It was just what the Bible said it was—a gathering of sinners, members of the race to the understanding of which the Fall supplies the most illuminating clue, and for the salvation of which the Gospel is the only hope. They would have thought ill of any minister who treated them otherwise or tickled their ears with shallower doctrine. From another point of view, they were local representatives of a nation composed of people like themselves—people, to be sure, who displayed all kinds of idiosyncrasies and oddities of character, who could moreover differ and dispute and divide with practised ferocity on circumferential aspects of religion itself, but people nonetheless like themselves in basic presuppositions and central faith.

In such a society the minister of religion needed to have no misgivings about his office and functions. If the Bible was religious authority materialized, he was that same authority vocalized. Even if the Bible gathered dust upon the parlour table, sign and symbol of latent presuppositions rather than of awakened and intelligent piety, he could be counted on to open it and read from it and thrust its message home. It was his proper and peculiar function so to do. The Catechism asked questions in cold print; he addressed them to you formidably in person and expected you to be word-perfect in the answers. Familiarity with the *Confession of Faith* as a printed document was not required of you, unless you were a divinity student or designated for the eldership. The *Confession* was rather like the Royal Navy, the sure shield of the believing community, an object of trust and pride, but not often visible. Yet Sabbath by Sabbath the minister preached the doctrines set forth in the *Confession* and he preached them squarely and confidently. He did not say, 'I venture to think . . .', or 'It seems to me . . .', and still less, 'If you will allow me to say so . . .', he said, 'This is the Word of God as it is received and is to be obeyed in His Church.' Sermons of the eighteenth and early nineteenth centuries give the impression of a caste of preachers completely at ease in their spirits concerning their office. They knew what it was their duty as preachers to do, and it was just what they were expected by their people to do: they had to preach the fundamentals of the faith as these are revealed in Scripture and had been reduced to dogmatic form in the confessional documents of the Church. The whole structure was marvellously massive and coherent, like a Norman castle. Like a Norman castle, too, it was unembellished and somewhat grim of aspect.

The difference between the situation thus cartooned and our own is the difference between snapshots of a city taken before and after a blitz: in the later one it is recognizably the same place as before, much standing secure as ever, if battered and scarred; but some buildings are precariously poised on ravaged bases and others in ruins. The main impression is one of confusion. It would be as far beyond my powers to describe or analyse our modern confusion as it is unnecessary for the purpose in hand. I shall only remind you of four features of it which you will find reflected among the people you will serve.

First, Sunday congregations are markedly smaller in numbers than they were in the heyday of the era just described. Some may interpret this despondingly as corroboration of an often quoted saying of Alfred North Whitehead:

> 'Protestant Christianity, so far as concerns the institutional and dogmatic forms in which it flourished for three hundred years as derived from Luther, Calvin and the Anglican Settlement, is showing all the signs of a steady decay. Its dogmas no longer dominate; its divisions no longer interest; its institutions no longer direct the patterns of life.'

In a more hopeful point of view it spells a healthy sifting, an unmasking of conventional religiosity. Here, however, let only one practical remark be made regarding any disappointingly small gathering of Christians: measured by a Christian calculus, it is still a great occasion, whatever mere arithmetic may suggest. It needs to be put plainly to every generation of divinity students that a minister grievously sins when he prepares less conscientiously for preaching to a handful than to hundreds, or lets himself become perfunctory and slovenly in his pulpit ministrations should his flock tend to diminish. Even carnal prudence might tell him that when he does so there will in all likelihood be fewer still next time. A moderate degree of faith might whisper to him that any given occasion may, under God, be decisive for one person and through that one for multitudes. A greater faith will be fixed on far horizons and ultimate evaluations, when every obscure fidelity will be seen to have sewn a stitch of gold thread in the coronation tapestries of heaven. Perhaps the best antidote to natural failings in this reference is fixedly to remember and well to ponder that word of Jesus which says, 'if two of you shall agree on earth as touching anything that they shall ask, it shall be done for them of my Father which is in heaven. For where two or three are gathered together in my name, there am I in the midst of them.'

A second feature of the modern congregation as compared with its predecessors in the pews is its less homogeneous character in respect of a theological grasp of the faith. In the old days a fledgling minister on his first flight of pastoral visitation might well be asked by one of his parishioners—possibly a strong-featured old lady with a mutch on her head and a Bible on her lap—to 'tak a rin ower the fundamentals'. She was not seeking enlightenment, be you sure: she was out to discover if 'the callant was soond'! She was nosing for a potential heretic! You need hardly fear that this kind of ordeal awaits you today. Where for long no clearly formulated and firmly articulated system of doctrine has been authoritatively administered, and where a vanished catechetical method has found no comparably efficient successor, it is hardly surprising that the old sturdy homogeneity should have given place to vagueness and variety of belief. Moreover, even if during the past half-century the doctrinal trumpets had been blowing with no uncertain sound, and blowing an identical fanfare *tutti con brio*, during the same period the air has been filled in the most literal sense with other voices confidently carrying rival doctrines into the ordinary man's ear as he sits by his fireside. It is little wonder if confusion should reign in the minds of intelligent churchmen, who are probably not less addicted to wireless listening than faithful to church attendance, and better acquainted with Bernal than with Barth. Recent years have doubtless witnessed an effort to revive doctrinal preaching: expositions of the Christian fundamentals are being given in occasional courses of sermons in many churches and on the wireless, and this has everything to say for itself over against round-the-year butterfly-preaching—a perpetual, incalculable fluttering from one flowery text to another. But this more solid style of preaching (which can easily, remember, if not artfully wielded, be a 'dreicher' kind of preaching, and make people long for the touch of a vanished butterfly) has done little as yet to counteract the theological looseness, one might almost say the theological lostness, of our time.[1]

Here let me say in the by-going that in his first pastorate, with profit to himself and his people, a young minister may well set before himself this among other vocational ambitions: having selected some dozen themes covering among them the central Christian doctrines, let him aim

[1] 'Theological lostness' is a different thing from irreligion, of course. Religion is one thing, its reflective formulation in a system of doctrine another. Where thoughtful people are concerned, theology is to religion what a cup with a handle is to the man who wants to drink from a deep river.

to have produced by the end of three or four years at least three sermons on each of them, the treatment being varied to suit different types of hearers; and let him put into the preparation of these discourses the best of his mind and the deepest of his spirit, the utmost of his labour and the finest of his art, rejecting everything tawdry and using for illustrative material only what will stand the wear of time. Carried through with perseverance and zest, a programme of this sort will at the very least have done something to safeguard a man's first essays in preaching against the least pardonable of faults—lack of substance and gravity.

In the third place, accompanying the theological looseness of our day and contributing directly to it, there is ignorance of the Bible and uncertainty regarding its authority. In a leaflet recently issued in preparation for the 'Bible Weeks' soon to be held in connection with the third jubilee of the founding of the British and Foreign Bible Society, this strong statement is made:

> 'The lack of knowledge of even the simplest truths of the Bible both inside and outside the Church is a well-known and admitted fact. Preachers, educationalists and others who have experience of this area of knowledge are at one in declaring that little or nothing can be taken for granted in knowledge of the Biblical message, and of its relevance to present-day life.'

But it is not only ignorance of the contents of the Bible which has to be reckoned with today, but also something which, in a country with a religious tradition like ours, is far more serious, namely, uncertainty regarding the authority of the Bible. The thoughtful layman is well aware that some profound change has taken place in the Church's attitude towards Scripture, but he finds it difficult to grasp what the change is, how much it implies, and where it is likely to lead. For his grandfather the Bible was a book of answers to life's problems, authoritative and divinely certified; for him it has become a book of problems to many of which there appear to be no authoritative answers—not even ecclesiastically authoritative, let alone divinely. Are the biblical narratives which are the carriers of the Gospel what they purport to be, and what his grandfather held them to be *in excelsis*—reliable accounts of historical events? Or are they admixed with symbolism, allegory, legend, myth and what not? Do they belong to primitive and obsolete ways of thinking? Have they been affected by bias and wishful thinking, coloured by childish fancies, corrupted by error? If so, how much? And who is to say how much? Is it to be Professor X who says one thing, or Doctor Y who says another, or the General Assembly which, however, on these matters does not nowadays say very much? Is he to believe his former minister, who was a near-modernist and rather coy about it, or his present minister, who is a near-fundamentalist and quite fierce about it?

Questions like these are the stock-in-trade of theological colleges so that their denizens, even if they cannot answer them, become gradually immunized to their upsetting effects. It is different with the layman. The upsetting questions reach him like the rumours that run about in wartime and that are not always dispelled by smooth official communiques. People who never had very strong religious constitutions succumb easily: you won't find them in church at all today. But you will find others of tougher spiritual fibre who, reverencing the Bible and having staked their lives on the truth of its teaching, are yet profoundly uneasy about the nature of its authority. They are like Polar explorers who waken up one morning to discover that their camp, instead of being pitched on the mainland, is adrift on an ice-floe.

We shall have to return to this aspect of the preacher's dilemma. Meanwhile only this: misgivings regarding the authority of the Bible, far from being automatically relieved by wider education and culture, tend to appear automatically as a by-product of these, except where the appropriate apologetic is being deliberately and vigilantly introduced into them. The reason is not far to seek: the wider education and culture of our day is predominantly scientific not only in content but also in temper and presupposition. But it is precisely modern science which has blown upon the traditional view of the Bible and necessitated some kind of reinterpretation of it. Until such a reinterpretation is as pervasive and persuasive as science itself, the progress of education can only add to the confusion about the Bible instead of helping to clear it up.

And that leads straight to this fourth point: whatever else our generation believes or disbelieves, it believes in science. For many the presuppositions of science have ousted all others and become the master-light of all their seeing. Some of them are Communists whose vision, as one ex-Communist has put it, is 'the vision of man's mind displacing God as the creative intelligence of the world'. Others who do not ally their scientific faith either with Marxist theory or Communist practice, yet equally with Communists hold it in divorce from any kind of theism.

In his recent careful and sensitive, if somewhat embarrassed, book on *Christian Faith and the Scientific Attitude*, Mr. W. A. Whitehouse thus describes the working creed of such people:

> 'Scientific thinking, bearing fruit in an all-pervading scientific attitude, promises to supply the resources by which man's economic standard of living can be raised, and all his capacities for good living can be developed. It is possible, according to this scientific faith, to organize life in a rational way so as to eradicate the international frictions leading to war and economic conflict. It is possible to produce and distribute man's worldly goods fairly and sensibly. For the first time in history, man will have the opportunity and the incentive to break free from the petty squabbles and sordid "necessities" which act today as a powerful brake on his development. Provided men can be cured of stupidity, human nature, like the world itself, will slowly reach perfection here in history. And the cure for stupidity is education in the scientific attitude.'[1]

Thousands of our contemporaries, being neither Communists nor fellow-travellers, but holding this kind of fundamental faith, are no longer in the Church. They have either deliberately severed any connection they may have had with it, or just drifted away from it. Only very occasionally will anything you say from the pulpit reach them, though a religious broadcast may now and then. But remember that the people left in the pews are all also profoundly affected by the buoyant and expanding scientific culture of our day. To quote Whitehouse again:

[1] *Op. cit.*, p. 28.

'The common man is inevitably inspired to try and think scientifically about his personal affairs, and, more and more, he pins his future hopes of happiness and success on "doing things scientifically". . . . When he is tangled up in personal and emotional difficulties, he knows perfectly well that a parson will say things to him which will only leave him battling with the same temptations after twenty years, so he turns to the psychiatrist for a "scientific cure". His very superstitions can be drawn into pseudo-scientific channels, as the more entertaining advertisements prove. Anything that purports to be a scientific prescription for radiant living commands his attention, even if he does retain enough sense to keep his money in his pocket. I am qualified to speak of him a little scornfully, for in describing him I describe myself.'[1]

What we Christians stand to gain or lose in this confused religious and cultural situation, what we ought to learn and what to unlearn, against whom we ought to be fighting and with whom we ought to be seeking alliance and on what terms—these are the great questions which our day has set to the Church's thinkers and leaders. In these lectures we shall not venture out into that wide uncharted ocean: hugging the shore, we shall only investigate one or two practical problems which the situation sets to the parish minister Sunday by Sunday.

★ ★ ★

It may seem to be taken lightly for granted in this lecture that all the Church needs to do in our day is to

[1] *Op. cit.*, p. 30.

put its house in order theologically—frame its faith anew in an up-to-date *Confession*, compile from it a new Catechism, and then set about indoctrinating its congregations on the post-Reformation model; and that all this is a task well within the Church's powers. But the main intention of the lecture is no more than to point the contrast between a former comparatively stable and tidy era and the vast upheaval of today amid which the Church must think and learn, as well as witness to what it believes. It would doubtless be grand if we could forthwith unloose three hundred fiery-tailed theological foxes among the Philistine corn; but how to catch the cohort of foxes, and how to get fire affixed to their tails, is the initial problem. Creeds and confessions are the outcome of religious revivals, not their efficient causes.

2

Preaching and Biblical Criticism

ONCE or twice recently I have heard the adjective 'post-critical' used to describe the era into which the Church is going forward, and used with an approving intention, as a Roman might have applied the term 'post-revolutionary' to the first phase of the Augustan age. Is your generation, in happy contrast with mine, to be congratulated in that you have warranty, as we at your stage had not, to regard the central battles of biblical criticism as fought to a victorious finish, and their results assessed and assimilated as much as needs be done? Can you get ahead with the real business of preaching the Gospel without being nagged by critical problems and the doubts which they sometimes engender? Dare we hope for a religious landscape no longer frowned on by the dark satanic mills of the International Critical Commentary?

In his last little book, *The Bible and Modern Scholarship*, Sir Frederic Kenyon passes under review the main developments of biblical criticism in the nineteenth and twentieth centuries. Then, after a searching examination of Bishop Barnes' book, *The Rise of Christianity*, he sums up the present position, as he sees it, as follows:

> 'The present generation is, to a greater extent than is often realized, better placed than its predecessors for

applying a sane criticism to the study of the Bible. It is free alike from the conventional assumptions of the pre-critical age and from the anti-traditional assumptions of the ultra-sceptical school which exhausted itself in the latter part of the nineteenth century. . . . It can strike a balance between these two extremes. It is in no way bound to assume that the tradition which satisfied uncritical generations is exempt from criticism, nor, on the other hand, that the anti-traditional view is always to be preferred, even though the bulk of the evidence is on the other side. Such a view is not merely a reaction against a period of excessive scepticism. It is ballasted by a considerable mass of ascertained fact, the result of archæological and literary research during the past fifty years. It can therefore approach the evidence from a new and firmer standpoint. It can give tradition its due weight. It is less free than it was to spin cobwebs out of its own inner consciousness; it has more facts to check them by, and has to form its theories under the salutary consciousness that more facts may at any time come to light to test them.'

The last sentences of the book, which refer to the literature of the New Testament, run as follows:

'What we are entitled to claim is that the books which we know as canonical were produced within some fifty years of the first century, and that the evidence for their text is in all essentials early and good. There is much room for diversities of interpretation, but the foundations stand sure, and we can without misgivings believe that we have in them the words of eternal life, to be interpreted and applied as best we can.'

Kenyon's broad conclusion is thus that biblical criticism, after sowing its wild oats in a way which caused its old-fashioned parents much anxiety, has settled down to sober habits, and there is no longer any need to fear that it will wreck the house in one of its outbreaks.

Alongside this estimate we may lay another, this time concerning the theological situation, which breathes a similar spirit of confidence as it looks to the Church's task in the immediate future. It is made by a recent Warrack lecturer, Mr. David Read, in his book on *The Communication of the Gospel:*

> 'We are not living in a period of great theological debate. Apart from the professional polemics of the theologians there is in non-Roman Christendom a most remarkable convergence of belief as to the fundamentals of the faith. This has been indicated not only in high-level ecumenical statements of faith, but in hundreds of conferences and missions where speakers are invited and books displayed for sale, on the assumption that a wide variety of speakers and writers from different denominations will have roughly the same point of view. They will be fashionably—and I hope genuinely—orthodox as to the major items of the Christian creed.'

In other words, we need no longer be seriously troubled by divisive controversies of the past. To be sure, theologians will be theologians, as boys will be boys, for whose high-spirited escapades due allowance must be made; but we can be confident that the Church has worked its way to an agreed understanding of the faith, and that the main residual problem concerns communication rather than either content or authority, a problem which Mr. Read proceeds to discuss with admirable freshness and force.

What is implied in his statement is made explicit in the leaflet about the 'Bible Weeks' already quoted. After the paragraph about the prevalent ignorance of the Bible, the document runs on:

> 'On the other hand there is this great asset—never before has there been such wide agreement among scholars of all denominations with regard to the main content of the biblical message. Differences of emphasis naturally remain. But in broad outline biblical teaching can now be lifted out of the older controversies to a positive proclamation of Him who is the Word made flesh.'

Further to all this, a not unimpressive measure of agreement has been reached in ecumenical circles regarding the methods by which the Christian message is to be derived from Scripture. I am thinking in particular of a series of conferences held under the auspices of the World Council of Churches and culminating up to date in one held at Wadham College, Oxford, in 1949, which issued a statement on 'Guiding Principles for the Interpretation of the Bible'. Its introductory paragraph contains the sentence, 'We have found a measure of agreement which surprised us all.' The headings of its four sections are these: 'The Necessary Theological Presuppositions of Biblical Interpretation,' 'The Interpretation of a Specific Passage,' 'The Discovery of the Biblical Teaching on a Specific Social or Political Issue,' 'The Application of the Biblical Message to the Modern World.' Under each of these headings a series of agreed findings is given, and the whole document is subscribed by some twenty scholars and teachers belonging to diverse confessional traditions, of whom many enjoy, and some are earning, a world-wide reputation.

If the evidence adduced is at all significant, it would seem that in respect of the three realms of study most directly contributory to the substance of preaching as distinct from its form—biblical criticism, dogmatics and hermeneutics—and therefore the realms most likely to occasion difficulty to the preacher should they be the scene of civil war, you are more happily placed than were your predecessors who emerged from the divinity halls thirty years ago or more. A sane and sober biblical criticism, enemy alike of obscurantist and sceptic; a neo-orthodoxy behind which is the authority of a *consensus doctorum;* an agreed hermeneutical method which will use the tools now provided by the scientists without endangering the faith once delivered to the saints—if these are what is meant by 'post-critical', a generation of Christian preachers is to be congratulated who set out under the shining of such favourable stars.

Without being by any means sure that the situation is in fact as happy as the foregoing estimate suggests, I am willing to take for granted that it is so. Indeed, the nearer the truth and the farther from wishful thinking the picture of a golden 'post-critical' age may be, the more forcibly I should wish to urge two considerations on those who will be preachers in it. They concern conditions which the legatees of the 'critical' era must fulfil if the new one is to be more than a barren revolt against its predecessor.

First, the positive gains of the 'critical' era must be jealously conserved and consolidated.

Let me ask, with apologies for so distasteful a reference, how you would answer the following question in an examination: What stands out as the chief fruit of biblical criticism since 1753, the year in which Astruc published his monograph, *Conjectures on the Original Memoirs which Moses appears to have used in composing the Book of Genesis?* One way of answering the question would be to give some account of the outstanding critical controversies of the past two centuries, to describe their swaying fortunes as this and that great scholar entered the lists, to point to their final outcome, and then to select this or that particular result as the most important of all. But all that, however learnedly done, would not earn more than an alpha minus, for it would have missed the name of the continent on the map and lost the shape of the wood among the trees. The biggest thing that has happened is simply that criticism of the Bible, based ultimately on the same scientific methods as have wrought vast changes in other fields of human life during the same period, has been legitimized and up to a point domesticated in the household of the Church with three inter-related results, and a possible by-product, of far-reaching importance.

(*a*) The first result may be indicated, more strikingly than exactly, by saying that a heresy about the Bible, analogous so far with docetism in the realm of Christology, has been exposed and repudiated. Biblical criticism has set it beyond all doubt—at least for those who believe that we have been given reason to reason by—that the Word Incartulate, the Word made Print, is not a sheerly divine book wearing a domino of human authorship, but a book in which cohere two natures, a divine and a human. Yet such an analogy serves only so far: it breaks down at the point where it is perceived that the human authorship of the Bible has not been exempted from human faults and failings, nor even supernaturally shielded from the malice of the printer's devil. A better analogy lies between Bible and Church, both divine-human realities belonging to two intersecting dimensions—the one a human, mundane, temporal dimension within which Bible and Church are proper objects of study and criticism by reason and science; the other a divine, eternal dimension in which Bible and Church appear as articles of faith and can only be understood by that faith which is the gift of God's Spirit. To the Bible as a fact within the human, horizontal dimension the scholar will rightly apply just such tools and techniques of study as to any other corpus of ancient literature, his primary supposition being that every sentence of every page of every manuscript of every book of the Bible has had an understandable historical provenance. Labouring thus, it has been the inestimable service of the critics to illumine the long and complex process by which this truly human body of literature came into existence, to characterize the various literary media used by the writers, and substantially to improve our knowledge of what they originally wrote and our understanding of what they meant by it. Granted that these labours have not led to agreed conclusions over the whole field of investigation but only to a central agreed territory pallisaded with question-marks, and granted even that certain crucial issues are still very much alive and open, the process has yet reached this broad result of first-class importance—the Bible has been brought into organic relationship with the modern scientific conception of history, a result as important for its right understanding as the assertion of the true humanity of Christ is for Christology.

(*b*) It is only shifting the perspective a little to say that critical scholarship has thus helped to translate the Bible, so to say, from stained glass into flesh and blood.

In one of her essays, *A Vote of Thanks to Cyrus*, Miss Dorothy Sayers tells in lively fashion how, for her, stained glass and flesh-and-blood coalesced into one world. It was when she discovered that Cyrus the Persian, whom she had always felt to be genuine flesh-and-blood, pigeon-holing him in her mind with the equally flesh-and-blood Greeks and Romans, was also a Bible character:

> 'I realized as with a shock of sacrilege that . . . he had marched clean out of Herodotus and slap into the Bible. *Mene, mene, tekel upharsin*—the palace wall had blazed with the exploits of Cyrus, and Balshazzar's feast had broken up in disorder under the stern and warning eye of the prophet Daniel. But Daniel and Balshazzar did not live in "the classics" at all. They lived in Church, with Adam and Abraham and Elijah, and they dressed like Bible characters, especially Daniel. . . . It was disconcerting. . . . I think it was chiefly Cyrus and Ahasuerus who prodded me into the belated conviction that history was all of one piece, and that the Bible was part of it.'[1]

On this evidence, one might almost say that Cyrus the Persian helped to write *The Man Born to be King* by translating the Bible for its future authoress into flesh-and-blood history from the never-never-land to which the

[1] In *Unpopular Opinions*.

stylisms of stained glass and the archaisms of the Authorized Version tend to relegate it, abetted in some unhappy cases by a preternatural honking in the pulpit. But what Cyrus did for the young Dorothy Sayers is precisely the service rendered by biblical criticism—it displays history as all of one piece and the Bible as part of it. It forbids us to use Elijah and David and the rest as marionettes dressed up for homiletic purposes in ideal virtues, and helps us to recognize them as our other selves, mortal men in the toils of history confronting the living God.

Remember that this is of crucial importance in the case of the Christian religion which ultimately stands or falls, not by the refinement of the ideas and ideals it presents, but by the historicity of the facts it attests. A Bible riding free in the sky of religious aspiration, a Bible starry with lofty thoughts—were it that and nothing more—would leave the world earthbound. It is because the Bible is all that and at the same time securely earthed—tolerant of being tied down here, there and everywhere into history, as the Lilliputians tied Gulliver to the ground by a thousand tiny ligatures—that it builds a firm bridge between the world and God.

(*c*) In doing these things, the biblical critics threw a bridge over a gap which threatened to cut off the Church from modern culture, and for that matter still threatens to do so.

In his book on *Miracles*, Mr. C. S. Lewis tells of a teacher of his—the man, he says, who 'taught me to think'—and this is how he introduces him:

'When a man who has had only the ordinary modern education looks into any authoritative statement of

Christian doctrine, he finds himself face to face with what seems to him a wholly "savage" or "primitive" picture of the universe. . . . Everything seems to presuppose a conception of reality which the increase of our knowledge has been steadily refuting for the last two thousand years and which no honest man in his senses could return to today. . . . The very man who taught me to think—a hard, satirical atheist (ex-Presbyterian) who doted on the *Golden Bough* and filled his house with the products of the Rationalist Press Association—thought in the same way; and he was a man honest as the daylight, to whom I here willingly acknowledge an immense debt. His attitude to Christianity was for me the starting-point of adult thinking. . . .'[1]

Let that picture of Mr. Lewis' teacher symbolize a host of men and women whom the Church lost and kept on losing so long as it actually defended, or seemed to be defending, intellectually disreputable positions, and refusing to reckon squarely with the new knowledge which science was gaining. The tragedy was that by resisting light on the horizontal plane of the Bible's bi-dimensional nature it was beclouding the other dimension in which the Bible has power to confront men with the living God. This didn't need to happen and didn't always happen. Professor Archibald Bowman once told me how as a young man, impressed and disturbed by attacks on the Bible which sought to discredit it altogether on the score of its 'primitive cosmogony', its 'childish tales of miracle' and so forth, he set out to read the Bible through from

[1] *Op. cit.*, pp. 83 ff.

beginning to end in order to come to a responsible personal judgment in the matter. As he fared along on this valiant enterprise, he found himself being quickly forced to a twofold conclusion: there was far more in the rationalist attacks than at that time the Church was willing to concede, and infinitely less than the attackers imagined. The man of reason and intellect in him soon came to realize that theories regarding the Bible in which he had been indoctrinated were untenable; the spiritual man in him, questing for the ultimates with the earnestness of later adolescence, was aware long before he had got through even the Pentateuch that the Bible, for all its 'primitive cosmogony' and the rest, is a strangely reverberating book, a book which has power to turn the tables on the critical enquirer. You sit on the bank and throw your line over its waters baited with your questions, and you may pull out some pretty little fish and possibly go home and write learned treatises about them; but one fine day something uncanny in the Bible swallows your hook and pulls you into the water for a life-and-death struggle. You venture to judge the Bible and up to a point it submits to your judgment, and then you may find the rôles reversed—you are in the dock and the Bible is the judge pronouncing sentence on you. A man of Bowman's intellectual and spiritual stature could reach his results on his own initiative; but many of his less richly endowed contemporaries could never have done so unless biblical criticism, exercised from within the Church, had thrown a bridge across to the place where they stood in their doubts and misgivings; in other words, unless the Church itself had demonstrated that revelation does not cease to be revelation when it is conveyed in earthen vessels, and that science need not be repudiated in order to retain faith, or faith in order to vindicate the scientific method.

But a bridge promotes two-way traffic, and so it was with this one: it enabled doubters to remain in the household of faith, and it opened a road to some acquaintance with scientific method for at least some of a class of believers whom this audience may possibly consider not unimportant—candidates for the Church's ministry. I do not know what it is like today, but in my day divinity students, who were mainly graduates in arts, were also graduates with first-class honours in ignorance of the natural sciences. At school and university our one brush with science had been in mathematics, which for many of us was like running your head against a wall in a black-out, but without even a flash of stars. Since I sat at the feet of the redoubtable Professor George Crystal, I have never been able to use with any sense of propriety the compound adjective crystal-clear. We had had an education, not without tears, but without test-tubes; an education in ideas, in values, in the humanities, but little if any confrontation with the hard facts of *natura naturata* to which the scientist enslaves himself in order to become its master. It was the scientific scholarship of the biblical critics which first woke some of us half-educated Masters of Arts to the possibility that Bachelors of Science might also be God's children. My own awakening from unscientific slumber came in the classroom of Professor Harry Kennedy, to whose memory I pay a most grateful and affectionate tribute. How he used to trounce writers who spin fancy theories out of their own clever heads! I can almost hear his voice saying, 'I need hardly remind you, gentlemen, that for these fanta*ss*tic conclusions there is not a *ssh*red of evidence in the New Testament. The most charitable judgment that can be passed on this prepo*ss*terous book is that its author is slowly drifting towards imbecility.'

Along with these three inter-related results we must take some account of the possible by-product earlier mentioned although, to be safeguarded against misunderstanding, the treatment would need to be more expansive and shaded than the scope of the present lecture allows.

One of the gains of the 'critical' era ought to be, whether or not it has in fact been, the avoidance of a wrong kind of pulpit dogmatism. Certainly the Church has something definite to say and must say it firmly, even in an age in which, as Dean Inge put it, 'Any stigma will do to beat a dogma.' But there is a kind of striving and crying aloud in the pulpit which is both offensive and self-defeating, because oblivious, I do not say of the spirit of the times, but of the motions of God's Spirit in our times. Wasn't it William James who somewhere spoke of 'reaching conclusions in the teeth of irreducible facts'? That is the kind of constraint which science imposes on its devotees, and the result has been a scientific meekness which bids fair, in one sense, to inherit the earth—if it does not succumb to vaulting ambition and overleap itself disastrously. There is a story of Jean Henri Fabre being watched by a gendarme as he lay stretched out on the ground intently observing some tiny insect, and being finally arrested as a suspicious character. That prone figure might well be taken as a symbol of the scientific spirit and the scientific method which are transforming civilization all about us. Certain noisy kinds of pulpit dogmatism compare ill with the humility, the quiet assurance, and even with the studied but expectant agnosticism of the true man of science. The adoption of scientific method in the realm of biblical criticism ought to teach us that dust thumped out of the pulpit-cushion is more likely to hide the Gospel from our contemporaries than commend it to them. After quoting one of Luther's onslaughts against Erasmus, Froude says this:

> 'Erasmus was not so destitute of religious conviction as Luther thought him. . . . So long as men believed in duty and responsibility to their Maker, he supposed that they might be left to think for themselves on theological mysteries without ceasing to be human, and it shocked him to see half the world preparing to destroy one another on points which no one could understand and on which both sides were probably wrong.'[1]

That is worth pondering. I confess I am afraid lest there be a reversion in a 'post-critical' era to a loud-mouthed authoritarianism, which may at bottom be a compensation for repressed uncertainties, and betoken unwillingness humbly to learn what God is seeking to teach His Church in and through the upheavals of our day. 'It is an old trait of human nature, when in a mist, to be very sure about its road,' says John Buchan.[2] But you will be better guides to people who have lost their way in the dark if you walk with a lit lantern than if you merely trumpet yesterday's sunshine.

The first main consideration, then, is that the positive and priceless gains of the 'critical' era must be jealously conserved and carried forward.

[1] Erasmus, *Life and Letters*, p. 401.

[2] In his *Montrose*, pp. 19–20.

In the second place, they must be far more widely distributed in the Church than has as yet been done.

Up to a certain point of time, so far as I can make out, there was no serious gap in respect of basic belief about the nature of Scripture between college and pulpit on the one hand and the pews on the other. What the college taught the pulpit preached, and what the pulpit preached the pew understood and believed. It was part of the strength of the old days that there was this uninhibited passage of thought throughout all parts of the Church: it gave the institution a cross-grain like that of tough timber. When the Higher Criticism began to make its way among the scholars, they did not at first regard it as esoteric knowledge for the clergy but as illumination for the whole Church. For example, Robertson Smith's twelve lectures on Biblical Criticism, eventually published as *The Old Testament in the Jewish Church*, were delivered in the first instance in Edinburgh and Glasgow to general audiences averaging eighteen hundred over the whole course. That was in 1880, and it may be taken as symptomatic not only of public interest in the apologia of a scholar who had lately been suspended from teaching but also of the cultural level of the Church of those days. Robertson Smith took for granted, and not mistakenly, that what he had been teaching to his students in Aberdeen was fit matter for a general audience of churchmen and would be appreciated by them. He could write in his preface:

'The sustained interest with which this large audience followed the attempt to lay before them an outline of the problems, the methods, and the results of Old

Testament criticism, is sufficient proof that they did not find modern Biblical Science the repulsive and unreal thing which it is often represented to be.'

About seventy years later, to institute a disproportionate comparison between the small and the great, I consulted an eminent scholar on the kind of course in Biblical Studies which might best serve graduates in Arts or Science who were preparing to be, or were already, teachers in our day-schools. The one clear-cut counsel he gave was this, 'Do not take up any critical questions with them,' seeming to take for granted that these constitute an improper or dangerous arena for laymen, even for university graduates. But there is better evidence than this straw in the wind that an unprecedented gap has opened up between what is being taught in the colleges and what is being received and believed in the pews.

Young people coming up to the universities are in general abreast of modern culture in the sense that their pre-academic training merges smoothly into the higher academic disciplines. In respect of the great majority of these disciplines there is no awkward gap or jolt between school and university, since both institutions accept the same presuppositions and move in the same realm of ideas. Yet these same young people, even where they have some knowledge of the contents of the Bible, bring up to the university, as a result of the interacting influences of home, school and church, the strangest medley of views about the nature of Scripture. Some of them—often the most earnest religiously—think that the Bible must not be criticized at all and belongs to a realm in which criticism is impious; others that it has long since been criticized out of court and belongs to a realm to which intelligence is alien. In between these two extremes are many who find the Bible an interesting but baffling book—a tangle of mountains among the foothills of which lie beautiful glens here and there which it is a morally and spiritually profitable exercise to explore, but beyond which you are bound to get hopelessly lost. In the case of comparatively few is there evidence of even a preliminary systematic training in the view of Scripture which, as the result of the gains of the 'critical' era, prevails and is presented in our theological colleges.

How has this come to pass—and in Scotland of all places, where we have ventured to pride ourselves on the nation-wide reach of a highly educated ministry over a highly educated democracy? It would take a full-scale enquiry to discover all the reasons in all their complexity, but I strongly suspect that a central one would be found to be a failure of the pulpit in my generation to do its full duty by the pew. As regards the whole matter of biblical criticism we have been too reticent, too timid, too little trustful of the intelligence of the ordinary man. We have forgotten that the Church's duty of instruction to its members, never less important than that of exhortation, becomes doubly important in an age of cultural upheaval, and that the pulpit is the keypoint of it. Topics neglected by the pulpit are topics unlodged in the general mind of the Church. The result has been a vicious spiral: the greater the reticence of the pulpit, the larger the leakage of uneasy intellectuals from the pew and the less flexible the mind of the residue; the larger such leakage and the stiffer the resultant mentality of the pew, the stronger the case for reticence and the heavier the premium on timidity.

And so the Church has come to suffer from a kind of schizophrenia, in that one part of it doesn't know what the other is thinking about the Bible, and would be horrified if it did.

More important than the question how this situation has arisen is the question how it can be corrected, and here I make three suggestions.

(*a*) The first can be made in a sentence or two, for it is only an underlining of what has already been said. Don't overhort your people, and don't underrate their intelligence: too much homily and too little instruction make a finally enervating diet. If the Church is to play its proper part, it must not be allowed to become a culturally stagnant enclave within the movements of our times; into its own proper outlook, the outlook orientated from the biblical insights, it must absorb all in modern culture that is congruent with them. God has promised His Spirit to His Church, but no monopoly of the Spirit. Indeed, it would seem to have been ordained that faith and reason, religion and philosophy, the 'sacred' and the 'secular', should be mutual critics within a common enterprise, like Prime Minister and Leader of the Opposition in the Parliamentary system; or to each other what the thorn in his flesh was to St. Paul, a needle to puncture self-satisfaction. In any case, the Church cannot rightly criticize what it has not first rightly understood.

(*b*) Where the mistake occurred, there it must be rectified, namely, in the ordinary week-to-week ministrations of the pulpit. Of course, in any well-organized congregation there will be a system of instruction of youth in Sunday Schools, Bible Classes and other gatherings of young people; and it will be a central responsibility of the minister to supervise it and to secure as far as possible proper grading, efficient staffing and adherence to a consistent and progressive scheme of instruction within which teaching about the nature of Scripture will be a staple ingredient. Time spent on training teachers and advising youth leaders on the syllabuses of fellowships and discussion groups will be better thus spent than on some shop-window kinds of ministerial activity. But the pulpit itself must always be the apex of the whole system: the pulpit itself must clinch what is being taught to the young people and carry it forward in ways appropriate to adult thinking; and nowhere does this need to be done with more candour and courage than in respect of what we have been discussing. Naturally, once a gap has opened, a measure of diplomacy must be used in attempts to close it; and even when that is done some types of hearer may be disturbed, and that will be unpleasant. But remember that the devil's favourite Sunday-morning entertainment is the sermon which does not cause a ripple of disturbance, intellectual, moral or emotional, to man, woman or beadle. If your pulpit motto is to be 'no disturbance!' you had better be a Trappist than a presbyter. There is evidence, however, that a warm welcome will be accorded to such preaching by people of immense importance to the Church today —thoughtful younger men and women who are uneasy about the Bible, and who want very much to be reassured about it without affront to their intelligence.

(*c*) The third thing concerns the manner in which this urgent task of the pulpit is to be discharged. An elementary point here is that every sermon you preach ought to rest on a sound exegesis of Scripture. Let that be the watermark of the paper you write on, and count it sin to use any other. This does not mean, I need hardly say, that to people hungering for spiritual bread you will offer critical stones, doling out J, E and P, for instance, as if these were the very latest thing in evangelical vitamins, and not just Moses dustily demosaicized. It does mean that you will regard it as an obligation of professional honour never to preach inconsistently with a sound critical exegesis.

But more is needed than this critical substructure. Set out in your first pastoral charge to accustom your people to study the Bible with a telescope as well as under a microscope. When you come to think of it, most of our preaching is microscopic in its treatment of Scripture: we generally take a tiny fragment for our text, sometimes a phrase of only a word or two, and we bend close over it, and peer into the depths of it, and so make what we can of it unto edification. This is the prevailing convention in sermon-making, and a profitable one, so rich, so auriferous, is the text of Scripture. I have heard a great sermon on the two words '. . . but God . . .', and a still greater on the less promising three words '. . . this is that . . .'.[1] But lest one good custom should corrupt the Church, lest this convention of tiny texts induce a permanently peering and myopic vision of the Bible, variant methods are needed. Get into the habit of occasionally taking a whole chapter as the basis of a single discourse. Occasionally give a lecturette on a whole book, your aim being as much to exhibit as to exhort—to tell what is known about its writer and history and how it articulates with Scripture

[1] V. Acts 2. 16. The subject of the sermon was 'The Identification of Religious Experience.'

as a whole, as well as to indicate in broad fashion its message for its own day and for ours. Some books of the Bible cry aloud for this large, synoptic treatment, and we are deaf to the cry because we are poring over their pages, tweezers in hand, absorbed in the hunt for some little bit of coloured thread to be teased out of the fabric, and then further teased down into three little fibrils, of which each must be delicately knotted up into a practical application. How refreshing it would be if, just once in a lifetime, one could hear a sermon on Ruth which was *not* based on the text, 'Intreat me not to leave thee', and which did *not* lead to certain obvious lessons on the virtue of fidelity, but which *was* based on the story as a whole, and which *did* lead into a discussion of the colour bar. If, as I guess, this kind of variant on custom and convention should prove to be as welcome to many of your flock as it is likely to prove a refreshing change to yourself, you may find it wise to introduce from time to time—not too frequently, but from time to time—a short course of this character covering parts of the Bible which belong together in special ways and which yield up richer meaning through being compared and contrasted with one another. At the very least once a year preach about the Bible, the whole Bible, the Word of God which makes wise unto salvation. But even then remember that eloquent panegyric of the Bible is only going to irritate the kind of person who wants first and foremost an apologetic, an answer to his perplexities and misgivings. It is really not very helpful to be given figures about the Bible's circulation and the number of languages into which it has been translated if you are really wondering whether, after all, *Das Kapital* is not a more reliable guide to life.

Putting all these things together, then, I suggest as one worthy aim for any given lustrum of your pulpit ministry—to educate your people in the general geography of this mighty continent which we call Holy Scripture, so that they may better know the character of the landscape, its great watersheds and watercourses, its catchment areas, its peaks and valleys, and not be acquainted merely with an assortment of beauty spots.

A last remark: the kind of preaching of which I have sought to commend a due infusion into a long-term pulpit-programme has one grand aim—to make Christ credible to a confused generation by rehabilitating in its regard the Book which testifies of Christ. It would be beyond measure satisfactory if Spurgeon's counsel to young preachers in his day were all that is needed in ours: 'Wherever you start from in the Bible, cut straight across country to Christ!' But Spurgeon was accustomed to audiences which had no serious worries about the Bible. It is different today. If you habitually cut straight across country to Christ, there are many who will disqualify you on the score of a false start.

3

Preaching on Miracle

A SIGNIFICANT difference between worship in the Church of Scotland and worship in the Church of England is that in the former you can guess pretty well, after a little experience in listening to sermons, what the minister will have to say about the text he announces (down even to particular illustrations which faithfully dog certain scriptures round the country until they are quite emaciated), but not so well what he may say in his prayers; whereas in the Church of England you know to a syllable what is coming in the prayers, while the sermon may surprise you. With my own ears I once heard a vicar begin a ten-minute utterance with the words, 'This morning I propose to give you the gist of two admirable discourses I happened to hear during my recent holiday.' And with my own ears I once heard an aged U.P. minister pray 'that the grand old institution of the Scottish Sabbath may never be secularized, continentalized, paganized, Anglicized.'

But you can never be sure what any preacher on either side of the Border will have to say about miracle, a circumstance not surprising if the wide variety of views advanced on the subject in publications and theological seminaries is remembered. The gamut may be divided into four registers. At one end of it, the end prolonged beyond the compass of the Church, there are those who hold not only that miracle is prescientific fairy-tale but also that religion itself, whose characteristic offspring miracle is, belongs to a passing phase of human evolution, being a schoolmaster to bring mankind to something higher, and therefore a menace to progress when it outlives its usefulness. No one has put this point of view more piquantly, or clothed it in a more attractive literary garb, than Schopenhauer did in his dialogue on Religion, from which the following catena of passages (all spoken by Philalethes) is extracted:

> 'Religions are like glow-worms: before they can shine it must be dark. A certain degree of general ignorance is the condition of every religion, and is the element in which alone it is able to exist. While, as soon as astronomy, natural science, geology, history, knowledge of countries and nations have spread their light universally, and philosophy is finally allowed to speak, every faith which is based on miracle and revelation must perish, and then philosophy will take its place.... Belief and knowledge bear the same relation to each other as the two scales of a balance: when the one rises the other must fall. . . . Perhaps the time which has been so often predicted is not far distant, when religion will depart from European humanity, like a nurse whose care the child has outgrown; it is now placed in the hands of a tutor for instruction. For without doubt doctrines of belief that are based on authority, miracles, and revelation are only of use and suitable to the childhood of humanity. . . . Religion is truth allegorically and mythically expressed, and thereby made possible

and digestible to mankind at large, for mankind could by no means digest it pure and unadulterated, just as we cannot live by pure oxygen but require an addition of four-fifths of nitrogen. . . . Meanwhile let us not give up hope that mankind will some day attain that point of maturity and education at which it is able to produce a true philosophy on the one hand, and accept it on the other. *Simplex sigillum veri:* the naked truth must be so simple and comprehensible that one can impart it to all in its true form without any admixture of myth and fable (a pack of lies)—in other words, without masking it as *religion.*'

What Schopenhauer thus expressed more than a century ago is brought up to date in balder style by Professor J. D. Bernal when he writes:

'. . . the history of scientific advance has shown us clearly that any appeal to Divine purpose, or any supernatural agency, to explain any phenomenon, is in fact only a concealed confession of ignorance and a bar to genuine research.'

In the next register of the scale come those who reject the conception of miracle without rejecting Christian theism, of whom Bishop Barnes in this country, and Professor Bultmann on the Continent, may be taken as outstanding representatives. In his *Myth in the New Testament*, Ian Henderson quotes the latter as going to the length of saying:

'It is impossible to make use of electric light and the radio, and, in case of illness, to claim the help of modern medical and clinical methods and at the same time to believe in the New Testament's world of spirits and miracles.'

There must be thousands of our contemporaries who, wittingly or unwittingly, hold this position. They may find it hard to understand just what Bultmann means by 'demythologizing'—a weakness on which perhaps even theological students may look leniently—but they will thoroughly understand and sympathize with him in his point of departure at which he serves himself heir to the critical methods of Liberalism and goes on to out-liberal the Liberals in his application of them.

But miracle has its doughty champions today, and that among eminent scholars for whom biblical criticism is a *sine qua non*. Our generation has seen a succession of important books which seek to restate the conception of miracle and justify it, not so much over against current scientific conceptions as in relation to them, so that the world of the New Testament and our world may be seen to be not two but one. I am thinking of books like A. G. Hogg's *Message of the Kingdom*, David Cairns' *The Faith that Rebels*, H. H. Farmer's *The World and God*, and C. S. Lewis' sparkling *Miracles*. These writers, critical scholars all, differ in the emphases they respectively lay on elements belonging to the concept of miracle; they differ more markedly when it comes to the question of denotation, to deciding which of the biblical narratives are authentic, and which spurious, instances of miracle, as they understand it; but they are at one in holding that miracle is a valid concept which must not be thrown to the scientists as though the Church were fleeing for its life and they a pack of pursuing wolves.

In the fourth and last register of the gamut come those who, accepting the Bible uncritically, accept its miracle stories unquestioningly, neither straining at gnats nor boggling at whales.

In such circumstances, it is an occasion of great interest when a text is announced from a miracle story, and not least if the preacher is not long out of college. There between him and hearers lies the Book whose pages gleam with stories of miracle almost as uniformly as its edges with gold-leaf—stories, *prima facie*, of a new world called in to redress the unhappy balance of the old; stories not of the inexorable working out of 'radiant laws, o'erruling human needs', whereby 'the cause to consequence proceeds', but of infinite love armed with infinite power stretching down from heaven to earth to avert disaster and confer salvation. I confess I am agog with interest on such an occasion, at least for the first few minutes, at least until certain things have become clear about the preacher's handling of the topic. Will he have anything to say which properly touches the miraculous aspect of the story, even if it be only what Montaigne calls 'a brisk hit in the nicest article of the question, leaving us to grope for the rest'? Or will he quickly sidle or shuffle off into the well-trodden paths of exhortation and the moralities? If he grapples with the miraculous aspect of the story, will what he says be vertebrate, displaying the bony structure of thought-out theory, or will he be as slippery as an eel? Will he give his audience credit for brains as good as his own, or will he treat them with the stooping benevolence of a radio uncle? Above all, will he be 'artless as the air and candid as the skies'—that quality which more than any other inspires confidence—or will he give the subtly disturbing impression of saying a little more than he has the right to say or considerably less than the congregation has the right to hear?

For anyone who knows a congregation from the inside, the drama of the occasion is heightened by the knowledge that in the pews two types of hearer will be represented, both of great importance in the present situation. There will be those who are able to believe in a naïve way, or who believe in a dogged and somewhat truculent way, whatever they find in the Bible and for whom the miraculous presents no special difficulty. If the Bible says that an axe once floated at the will and word of a prophet of God, then so it was and what else needs be said about it? In particular, they accept the recorded miracles of Jesus as supernatural deeds natural to the Incarnate Son of God. If such people are troubled at all, it will be when the preacher walks delicately in the neighbourhood of miracle, like an exegetical Agag smelling danger. Then they may wax indignant like the old beadle in Hamish Hendry's poem:

> 'As for the Bible, if you please,
> He thinks it's true,—in twa degrees;
> Some pairt is chalk, some pairt is cheese;
>   But he'll engage
> To riddle oot the biggest lees
>   Frae ilka page!
>
> No that he says sic things straucht oot;
> Lord! he's as sly's Loch Leven troot;

But here wi' Science, there wi' Doot
He crams his sermons;
Thrawin' the plainest text aboot
To please the Germans.'[1]

But another kind of hearer is included in every Christian audience today—the believer, or would-be believer, whose mind has been dipped or steeped in modern science, habitually uses scientific concepts and techniques in his own vocation, and may perhaps moreover know a good deal about modern biblical criticism. Such a hearer may be ready enough to accept ethical teaching which the preacher extracts from the sacred text, but from the nature of his mind and education he cannot help asking whether the miracle story itself is not a kind of Christmas tree—a fir-sapling once grown in good earth, but now sawn off from its roots and dressed out in tinsel and baubles. In proportion as he is earnest in Christian faith and anxious to be intelligent about it as well, he will wish to know what the preacher thinks and believes about these matters, and in the same measure irritated if the discourse veils it. What is to be done in this confused situation?

Some men take the line of least resistance by giving the whole realm of miracle a wide berth in their preaching, and perhaps even also in their choice of Scripture lessons. Is there not enough Christian truth in all conscience, they ask, on which to preach profitably without bringing in these difficult topics? But it is the Bible itself which brings

[1] From *The Beadle's Lament* in John Buchan's anthology of Scots vernacular poetry, *The Northern Muse*, p. 230. The poem is a little classic of its kind, reflecting most racily the transition period between the old Calvinism of Scotland and the modern scene.

in these topics; and if a man is silent about them for the rest of the year, can he be silent about them on Easter Day? As it seems to me, a preacher's silence on the subject of miracle resembles a Victorian parent's silence on the subject of sex: it is the embarrassed evasion of a duty rather than the solution of a problem. At a critical point he is failing to play his part in the apologetic task of our day—the commendation of the Bible to mind as well as to heart, to reason as well as to conscience and affection. Yet it would be better to say nothing than to speak cagily, merely hinting at a realm of knowledge and belief about which you propose to keep your own counsel. Indeed, a man's first principle in this whole field should be to pitch his utterance for the ear of the most acute and critical intelligence in his congregation, and to say with candour and simplicity just what he holds to be true. For the day on which he is going to preach about miracle let him forget Luther's advice always to preach to the washer-woman in the back pew, and let him have specially in mind the keen-witted lawyer, or the science teacher, or what Marcus Dods once called 'those wasps of students'. It will not matter very seriously if once in a while the washerwoman is a trifle bemused, so long as she feels that something big has been going on; but it will matter much if the lawyer and the teacher and the wasps go away from church feeling that on a perplexing subject the pulpit has had nothing at once relevant and serious and honest to say. That is why I find it difficult to agree altogether with what Dr. Henry Sloane Coffin advises in his lectures on preaching:

> 'The pulpit is usually not the place to deal with the question of the historicity of any biblical narrative.

That can be done, when necessary, more wisely in a less formal setting where there can be discussion and the give and take of question and answer.'[1]

I should be happier about this counsel if I could be sure that such less formal meetings would in fact take place and be attended by the same people as normally attend canonical services. But is the fact not that any special gatherings for Bible study, if held at all, are usually sparsely attended and that by the people who least need instruction because they are the best equipped for study on their own initiative? The canonical services of the Church are a minister's principal and irreplaceable teaching opportunity, and it ought to be used for the treatment of any biblical topic which presents difficulties to his people. This does not necessarily mean that he should give formal courses of sermons on the miracles of the Old and New Testaments, although he might do worse; but he ought at any rate to give the subject a fair place in his pulpit programme over a given period, and so handle it that after a year or two his people are left in no doubt as to what he believes.

Taking candour and honesty for granted as an overruling principle, I suggest that three general aims ought to govern the preacher's treatment of miracle stories.

(1) The most important is that the treatment should enshrine the essential biblical and religious meaning of miracle, which is epitomized in Isa. 59. 1: 'Behold, the Lord's hand is not shortened, that it cannot save; neither

[1] *What to Preach*, p. 39. Published in 1926 (by Hodder and Stoughton, London), this volume remains one of the most valuable aids to preaching which a young minister can possess.

his ear heavy, that it cannot hear'. Whatever its provenance, every miracle story in the Bible has as its ultimate theme the power of God to reveal Himself as the righteous Redeemer, a very present help in time of trouble to those who put their trust in Him; so that any treatment of the miraculous will be a failure and a fiasco which does not send away a congregation with the faith renewed in its heart that 'God never yet forsook at need the soul that trusted Him indeed.'

But a good deal needs to be said at this point regarding the relation of the miracle stories as a whole to Scripture as a whole and, in particular, regarding the question whether Scriptural truth is accredited by them in much the same way as a foreign ambassador is accredited at the Court of St. James by the letters he carries from his government. In *The Book of the Twelve Prophets*, Sir George Adam Smith tells of an Arab chief, who wished to consult a distant soothsayer as to the guilt of a daughter.

> 'But before he would trust the seer to give him the right answer to such a question, he made him discover a grain of corn which he had concealed about his horse. He required the physical sign before he would accept the moral judgment.'[1]

Are the biblical miracles the physical signs on the strength of which the biblical message about God may be accepted, and in the absence of which it would be untrustworthy? To use one of Principal Cairns' images, are the miracle stories like seals attached to a business document rather than part of the document itself?

[1] *Op. cit.*, p. 15.

To these questions the answer must be that the Bible is a self-accrediting book, of which miracle is an integral element. One might put it in this way: the Bible has authority at all because it introduces us to a 'hard' world, a world which refuses to yield before us as though the only reality were our own will to be and to do and to enjoy. This world of the Bible proves to have a substance as resistant and edges as cutting as has the material world: as you move about in it, you find yourself blocked and opposed by an 'other', accrediting itself as real through its resistance to the motions of your spirit, just as matter does through its resistance to the motions of your body. In either world you may try to evade the resistant aspect of the obtrusive reality, or you may boldly advance against it with the intention of subduing it to your own purposes, so that your own will may be the only significant reality; but whether you do the one thing or the other, it is brought home to you over and over again that there is something real there over against you. In the one case, it is that reality which the senses discern and which elicits their activity—the tangible, measurable, ponderable, propellable world; a world, to be sure, which has proved to be wonderfully docile and plastic to man's ambition, yet which retains its own peculiar 'hardness', sometimes lying brutely and inertly obstructive, sometimes appearing to display what the Germans call *die Tücke des Objekts*—the mischief of matter—sometimes coming back very sharply at you, even to the point of maiming or killing you, and never leaving you in any practical doubt about its reality. Even a solipsist metaphysician is apt to address a stone in strong terms when he stubs his toe hard against it, just like a navvy.

In the case of the Bible, the 'hard other' is the reality of God, the God and Father of Jesus Christ, who bars your way and will not let you pass, who pens you into a corner and will not let you free until you have submitted to His sole Lordship. Now, this is pictorial and quasi-mystical language, and I can quite understand how an agnostic mathematician, were he here present, would be saying to himself, 'I don't understand a word of it!' And this is exactly what I should have to say to him were he to try to convey to me the basic truths of mathematics in the language appropriate to them. But I should be much disappointed if what has been said were a meaningless signalling to this audience, which may be presumed to have had some experience of the Bible's intrinsic power to make men aware of God as real. The authority of the Bible derives solely and entirely from this power, and is impregnably self-subsistent: nothing that the Church can say—no dogma about inspiration—can add in the slightest way to it; and nothing that philosophers or scientists can say—no dogma based on extra-biblical presupposition—can subtract in the slightest way from it.

But the God whom we confront in the Bible is a miracle-working God. By this is not simply meant the truism that miracle stories are an element in Scripture which we have no right to subtract or suppress. It is meant that, even were we to do that, we should still confront One whose nature it is to do wondrous things in mercy and judgment. The miracle stories in the Bible do not serve to establish what without them would have been absent: they are not like the tinsel and baubles which a sombre fir tree could not have produced from its own sap. Rather are they ideographs of the Bible's message about God, pictures which properly belong to the letter-press and appropriately vivify it. For the aspects and qualities of the Divine nature which form the matrix of miracle are the substance of the message of both the Testaments.

The God of the Bible is the Creator. The adjective creative is often used in a diluted sense of human artistic originality, but in the Bible creation is the divine prerogative, the exercise of which excites awe rather than admiration. Hence the sublimity of passages like the fortieth of Isaiah or the thirty-eighth of Job in which the writers contemplate the mysterious hinterland of absolute creative energy lying behind the majestic coastline of nature.

Again, the God of the Bible rules over the entire creation in entire personal freedom. He is no powerless prisoner within His own universe, like a mediæval baron who has fallen into the bottle-dungeon of his own castle, or like the inventor of some elaborate strong-room on whom its door has swung to. He is the God who can say, 'I will work, and who shall let it?'; who 'doeth according to his will in the army of heaven, and among the inhabitants of the earth: and none can stay his hand, or say unto him, What doest thou?'; of whom Jesus could say at the supreme crisis of His earthly life, 'Thinkest thou that I cannot now pray to my Father and he shall presently give me more than twelve legions of angels?'

Once again, since the freedom of the God of the Bible is personal freedom, it is exercised with a purpose, in character. It is not a purpose or character which reveals itself to any careless or casual glance at the created universe: it is not written so large over nature and history that it cannot be missed or blinked. Rather it resembles those portraits of the Stuarts, painted on the 'anamorphosis' principle, which Royalists sometimes carried in the days of the Protectorate, and Jacobites in the early days of the House of Hanover. Looked at by the natural eye, they were unrecognizable caricatures; but seen in mirrors which corrected the distortions of the royal likeness, they were faithful images of the features of King Charles I or Prince Charles Edward. Seen in the natural vision of even highly cultivated and earnest-minded men, nature and history do not speak compellingly of either righteousness or love: their compelling features are rather mystery and tragedy; but viewed in the light of the story which culminates in Christ, and viewed with the new eyesight which Christ confers, life's mystery and life's tragedy are seen to gleam with the steel of Divine righteousness and glow with the fire of Divine love.

Yet again, God's purpose, as the Bible reveals it, is prosecuted with utter reliability and infinite resourcefulness. It is a fruitful exercise to follow through in a large concordance of the Bible the entries under the words covenant and faithfulness. How nobly phrases such as 'an everlasting covenant', 'the faithful God that keepeth covenant and mercy', 'I will remember my covenant', resound through the Old Testament, as they are taken up by one prophetic voice after another and bring consolation and courage to successive ages of Israel! How spacious is its language when it speaks of the Divine faithfulness! 'It reaches unto the clouds,' says one Psalmist—'soars to the very skies,' as Moffatt dynamically translates it; 'it is

firmly fixed in heaven,' says another; 'it is unto all generations,' says a third. Then comes One of whom St. Paul says that 'in him the promises of God are Yea, and in him Amen'; whom the writer to the Hebrews calls 'a merciful and faithful High Priest' and St. John in the Revelation calls 'the Amen, the faithful and true witness, the origin of God's creation'; the One who corroborates all that God ever promised, signing and sealing it in His life's blood, so that the men of the New Testament can call down all the corridors of time, 'God is faithful!'

An utterly reliable God, yes, and an infinitely resourceful God whose power is inexhaustible and His ingenuity untold! 'He can of these stones raise up children to Abraham,' says John Baptist; 'he can do exceeding abundantly above all that we ask or think,' says St. Paul; 'with him all things are possible,' says Jesus.

But when you have put these things together—the freedom of the Creator to rule over His creation in righteousness and love with utter constancy and infinite ingenuity—you have already in your hand the religious substance of the concept of miracle. And wherever miracle is impugned, you will always find that one or another attribute of God, as we confront God in the Bible, is being denied either openly or implicitly—His freedom to act in righteous love, or His willingness so to act, or His resourcefulness in such action.

As you would expect, living religion experiences what biblical theology so clearly presents. In a vivid passage Karl Heim voices this truth in relation to prayer, that essential activity of living religion in which the human spirit, being united by faith to the Uncaused

Cause, is lifted up out of its chains into the freedom proper to it:

> 'It is part of the essence of prayer to have the certainty that the whole of world-history, from the solar orbits to the oscillations of the electrons, lies in this moment in the hand of God like soft clay in the hand of the potter. He can make of it what He wills. No sparrow falls from the roof without His will. Whether the form of the world changes or remains the same, it does not happen from causal necessity, but because God wills it so. In everything that may befall me in the next moment, I have to deal not with dead matter, with laws of nature, nor with men, but only with Him. Always I stand before the simple choice between Him who draws me upward, and the adverse force which wants to draw me down. . . . Miracle is the victory of God in this strife of spiritual powers. Everyone who prays knows that victory is possible at any moment and in any situation.'[1]

And this assurance is reinforced in the life of Christian obedience among all earth's cares and contradictions which is the other side of prayer, to which the man who has well prayed returns with a more disciplined purpose, and of which the deepest motive is the will to fill up what is lacking in the sufferings of Christ. Mr. Lewis pushes this truth to its extreme limit, and heavily emphasizes its negative counterpart, when he writes:

> 'You are probably quite right in thinking that you will never see a miracle done. . . . If we were heroic

[1] *The New Divine Order* (S.C.M. Press, 1930), p. 50.

missionaries, apostles, or martyrs, it would be a different matter. But why you or I? . . . Miracles and martyrdoms tend to bunch about the same areas of history—areas we have naturally no wish to frequent.'[1]

This is true enough, no doubt, so little heroic, so fleshly frail is our normal discipleship. Yet, taken as a whole, the passage fails to reckon, I consider, with an area of workaday obedience short of high heroism but capable of being tinged with its quality, to which miracle may be revealed, not in noontide splendour, yet in vagrant gleams such as visit highland hillsides and announce through mist and cloud the unconquered power of the sun. Who that has carried obedience to its deeper and more costly levels, even if only in homely fields, had not been aware of finely-pointed conjunctures of outward circumstance which look like the response of a person, and powerfully suggest nice contrivance by a co-operating will? It will not do to discount such incidents as in themselves petty or paltry: light which pierces through a pinpoint aperture is still the authentic light of the sun. Neither will it do to dismiss the religious interpretation of them as necessarily fantastic, unless you are prepared to dismiss also as fantastic the saying, 'If any man will do his will, he shall know of the doctrine, whether it be of God.'[2]

[1] *Miracles*, p. 201.

[2] Some will hold that this paragraph fails to observe a necessary distinction between special providence and miracle proper. (Cf., e.g., *The World and God*, p. 120 ff.) But the distinction seems to me somewhat artificial, since awareness of God's succour can be vivid on either side of it.

The first principle, then, in this realm of preaching is that it should unmistakably contain the biblical and religious essence of miracle, that 'the Lord's hand is not shortened, that it cannot save: neither his ear heavy, that it cannot hear.' By its due observance, simple believers are encouraged to face life's mysteries and tragedies in the faith that 'God is their refuge and strength, a very present help in trouble.' Yet, by itself, this will not loosen the knot of our special modern problem in preaching miracle, the presence in the pews of many for whom miracle has become but the fairy-tale of childish piety, to be discarded along with Santa Claus and the hugged toys of the nursery. I remember commending *The Faith that Rebels*, at the time of its publication, to a friend of mine, a highly cultured headmaster and a loyal churchman. His verdict was summary: 'A gallant failure!' No preaching on miracle can be considered adequate today which fails to reckon with this type of hearer and to meet him on the ground of his objections and perplexities. This means, I think, that two further principles should govern our pulpit handling of the topic.

(2) An element of apologetic needs to be introduced—some exposition, that is to say, of the reasonable basis of what is believed. In any single sermon there may only be room for Montaigne's 'one brisk hit in the nicest article of the question', but if you are dealing with the topic in a connected series of discourses, it ought to rest on a firm apologetic foundation. And your material for this had better be collected now: scrabbling and scribbling it up on the battlefield of an active pastorate will hardly make for sound building. You will find rich quarries in books

already mentioned, of which Farmer's will especially reward the strenuous and patient toiler, and Lewis's mightily entertain while it instructs.

Properly speaking, it is no business of mine to dabble in apologetics in these lectures, yet I venture to set up one or two fingerposts to lines of treatment which may be found profitable.

(*a*) It is the boast of our day that the scientists can effect transfigurations in the body of nature in ways more and more astonishing in proportion as increased knowledge and improved techniques are brought to bear upon it. But the very brilliance of scientific successes of this kind may easily obscure two aspects of the situation in which they have been achieved, both being highly relevant to a consideration of miracle. The first is that the familiar objects of the natural world—pebbles, mud, fungi, what not—which seem so fixed and concrete in their being, so humbly contented with their own individualities, have been found to be of an infinite complexity, each a world within the world; to be, moreover, beneath their seeming stolidity, of a gossamer fineness and fluidity of texture by virtue of which new patterns can be imposed upon them. Let me give a very crude illustration of what is meant. To most of us a peanut is just what a primrose was to Peter Bell. We might say:

> A peanut in its wrinkled shell
> A simple peanut is to Bell,
> And it is nothing more.

But it would seem that there is very much more in a peanut than meets the casual, unscientific eye. Here is his own account of how George Washington Carver, the negro scientist, came to concentrate his attention on this guttersnipe of a nut:

> 'I asked the Great Creator what the universe was made for. "Ask for something more in keeping with that little mind of yours," He replied. "What was man made for?" "Little man, you still want to know too much. Cut down the extent of your request, and improve the intent." Then I told the Creator I wanted to know all about the peanut. He replied that my mind was too small to know *all* about the peanut, but He said He would give me a handful of peanuts. And God said, "Behold, I have given you every herb bearing seed, which is upon the face of the earth . . . to you it shall be for meat . . . I have given every green herb for meat: and it was so." I carried the peanuts into my laboratory and the Creator told me to take them apart and resolve them into their elements. With such knowledge as I had of chemistry and physics I set to work to take them apart. I separated the water, the fats, the oils, the gums, the resins, sugars, starches, pectoses, pentosans, amino acids. There! I had the parts of the peanuts all spread out before me. I looked at Him and He looked at me. "Now you know what the peanut is." "Why did You make the peanut?" The Creator said, "I have given you three laws; namely, compatibility, temperature and pressure. All you have to do is to take these constituents and put them together, observing these laws, and I will show you why I made the peanut." I therefore went on to try different combinations of the parts under different conditions of

temperature and pressure, and the result was what you see.'[1]

The result would seem to have considerably exceeded the remit that 'to you it shall be for meat', for, according to Carver's biographer,

> 'from this storehouse of wonders, combinations in many curious and uncommon forms poured in a never-ending stream . . . a dozen beverages, mixed pickles, sauces (Worcestershire and chili), meal, instant and dry coffee, salve, bleach, tan remover, wood filler, washing powder, metal polish, paper, ink, plastics, shaving cream, rubbing oil, linoleum, shampoo, axle grease, synthetic rubber . . .'[1]

Even this crude, pre-atomic illustration may suffice to remind us that matter is 'a storehouse of wonders', an Aladdin's cave full of hidden treasure and—this is the pertinent point here—very far from explored as yet in its inmost windings and recesses.

And the illustration brings into focus also a second aspect of the situation even more easily overlooked amid the excitements of crowding new scientific discoveries and inventions. It is simply that science is a different thing from omniscience, and man's intelligence a limited instrument. Centuries after Newton, the corpus of scientific knowledge is still a pebble on the ocean's strand; at their most refined, the techniques of research are still uncouthly incommensurate with the tenuous fineness of their object, a ditch-digger's fingers handling cambric; and at their grossest, our modern engines and instruments—foundries and factories, compressors and cyclotrons—are monsters

[1] Rackham Holt, *George Washington Carver*, pp. 226–228.

beside which a dinosaur would look a masterpiece of daintiness.

But if man's childish crudeness can wonderfully subdue nature to his chosen ends, how much more shall not God be able to exploit and manipulate His own creation to advance His purposes? Set in this perspective, the question of the possibility of miracle boils down to the question of the existence of God.[1] Jeremiah's apostrophe, 'Ah Lord God! behold, thou hast made the heaven and the earth by thy great power and by they stretched out arm; and there is nothing too hard for thee', will be pointless only for such as parody God into man, whose liturgy begins, 'O man, how excellent is thy name in all the earth! Who hast set thy glory above the heavens. . . . When I consider thine inventions, the work of thy fingers, the aeroplanes and atomic bombs which thou hast made, what is God that I should be mindful of him, or the Son of God that I should reverence him?' But for those who believe in the God of the Bible, the 'miracles' of science are no more than *maquis* exploits compared with what the omniscient and omnipotent Liberator is eternally able to do. Instead of discrediting miracle, they only adumbrate it in a blurred and blundering way.

[1] This is the conclusion which Professor Ian T. Ramsey reaches by a much more arduous route of argument in his *Miracles, An Exercise in Logical Mapwork*, p. 23. 'We will rightly be suspicious of any denial of miracles which comes because a particular metaphysical language has no room for the word, especially if a particular language is the result of trying to do metaphysics with one language model. But such philosophical blundering or prejudice must not blind religious people to the truth that ultimately the defence of miracle is the defence of a personally active God. They stand or fall together.'

(*b*) There is thus no more contradiction between miracle and science than between poetry and prose, and as little reason that they should live a cat-and-dog life as that beetles should be at feud with aeronauts. Miracle is the occasion when the Supreme Artist, whose command of brush and medium is complete, does with an easy turn of the wrist what the earnest apprentice vainly strives to do with knotted brow and straining fingers. And when, in given situations, God chooses to bring into play resources hidden deep in the Aladdin's cave of nature, He no more breaks the laws of nature or revokes nature's witness to His constancy than the scientist does when from the black and acrid body of coal-tar he conjures delicate perfumes and subtle colours unknown before. In a book published long ago (which, by the way, anticipates in essentials the line taken by C. S. Lewis) Horace Bushnell made this point in the following words:

> 'Two things are manifestly wanted and one as truly as the other: viz., nature and the supernatural; an invariable scientific order, and a pliant submission of that order to the sovereignty of wills, human and divine, without any infringement of its constancy. For if nature were to be violated and tossed about by capricious overturnings of her laws, there would be an end of all confidence and exact intelligence. And if it could not be used, or set in new conjunctions by God and His children, it would be a wall, a catacomb, and nothing more. This latter is the world of scientific naturalism, a world which might answer well enough for the housing of manikins, but not for the exercise of living men.'[1]

[1] Horace Bushnell, *Nature and the Supernatural*, published in 1864.

And Edwin Muir has compressed the same truth into four lines of a Christmas poem—an apt illustration in the present context of the swift miracle of poetry which mocks the plodding gait of philosophers and theologians:

> 'The star that left the starry throng
> Caused no confusion in the night.
> Nor strayed to prove his brothers wrong,
> But told that all the stars were right.'[1]

(*c*) Another apologetic consideration concerns the Person of Jesus Christ. Few today have much difficulty in accepting the moral miracle of His personality. Listen to this:

> 'He was too great for his disciples. He was like a terrible moral huntsman digging mankind out of the snug burrows in which they had lived hitherto. Is it any wonder that men were dazzled and blinded and cried out against him? Even his disciples cried out when he would not spare them the light. . . . For to take him seriously was to enter upon a strange and alarming life, to abandon habits, to control instincts and impulses, to essay an incredible happiness. . . . Is it any wonder that to this day the Galilean is too much for our small hearts?'[2]

Of the multitude of people who would agree with these words of H. G. Wells, I know of none who goes on to argue, 'Yes, the biblical records point to a personality in Jesus higher than is natural to humanity; but, of course,

[1] The poem appeared in the Christmas number of the *Observer*, 1952.

[2] H. G. Wells, *The History of the World*.

for that very reason they must be false, and he cannot have existed as described.' Yet the odd thing is that some people who acknowledge the transcendent personality of Jesus sometimes do argue that way about the miracle stories which are part of the New Testament narrative. 'Until we have seen such things happen elsewhere,' they say, 'and until we can do them ourselves under laboratory conditions, we must take leave to doubt that they happened as described.' But surely the logic of science itself should lead us to expect new and unique results from the entry into a familiar situation of a new and unique factor, namely, from the life in a human body of a spirit belonging to a plane higher than is natural to our morally frail humanity. Jesus Christ, whose meat it was to do His Father's will and whose fellowship with God was unclouded by the sense of guilt, a relationship of eager intimacy and joy; who loved his fellowmen without prudent limit or slyly calculated margins to safeguard comfort or safety, so that at the last He died for them—is it so incredible a thing, rather is there not a large reasonableness satisfying to our human sense of fitness, that to such a personality, united in such a fellowship with nature's Creator, the natural world should prove subservient and responsive in new and unique ways?

(3) It remains to advance a third principle which must be applied no less resolutely than the other two. All that has been said does not mean that when miracle is welcomed at the door, reason must fly out of the window, and science be hustled into the cellar, lest their manners disgrace the occasion. On the contrary, reason and science must strictly police the approaches to the door, in order that gate-crashers may be turned away and impostors

arrested. Indeed, there is no aspect of religion in respect of which reason and science have a more responsible part to play than the miraculous, since it is precisely here that faith is most apt to degenerate into credulity, and wishful thinking to oust sobriety of judgment.[1] Equally with the wildest extravagances of pagan myth and mediæval hagiology, the biblical miracle narratives are allegations of event, of happenings beneath the sun within the sense experience of men, regarding the credibility of which reason and science have their own right to a voice. When the Vatican examines claims to canonization, these are contested before the tribunal of cardinals by an official whose duty it is to expose every weakness in them. While this functionary is popularly known as 'the devil's advocate', very properly the Roman Church officially entitles him 'the promoter of the faith'.

To speak less generally, we must discriminate among miracle narratives by applying to them the methods basic to literary, artistic and historical criticism, as well as to the physical sciences. Under this kind of scrutiny they may be assigned to different categories: some narratives may be judged to be instances of legend or idealized history; others, instances of symbolic poetry; still others, the results of a tradition modified and embellished in the course of its transmission; and so forth. It would be as idle to expect unanimity of judgment in this difficult field as in questions of artistic criticism, and foolish to reject the whole procedure as worthless because it cannot claim to be infallible or pronounce with certainty in every case.

[1] Farmer's analysis of this danger in *The World and God* is very searching. The relevant passages will be found by reference to the word *Eudæmonism* in the index of subjects, p. 309.

Were this a lecture on miracle, and not merely one on preaching on miracle, it would be necessary at this point to go very fully into this difficult matter of the criticism of miracle narratives, and to try to frame a code of critical canons. I count myself fortunate in being absolved from such a task, and able in good conscience to confine myself in conclusion to two things: first, a confession of personal belief; and then three brief practical counsels.

I believe that from the crucible of criticism there emerges a residue of miracle narratives untainted by 'eudæmonistic corruption', which must be accepted either as plain history or as something which may be called poetic history—the event in which poetry and history have mysteriously mated to bring to birth what is at once sober fact and profoundest symbol and creative prophecy.

Finally: (*a*) never forget that the miracle narratives belong to two realms, as does the whole Bible—the realm of faith and revelation and eternity, and the realm of sight and science and history. It will not do today to treat them as though they belonged to one only: if you try to do that, on the one side of the alternative you will be apt to bolster credulity, and on the other to beggar faith.

(*b*) Let your handling of any miracle story leave your hearers in no doubt as to whether you believe it to be a credible record of historical event or something different and, if a different kind of narrative, what kind of one. As we have seen, this may get you into trouble in some quarters, but I believe it will be much welcomed by a very important section of the Church and many who hesitate and hover on the fringes of it.

(*c*) But remember that miracle is a religious concept, and that in the last resort it is faith, the eye of religion, which must pronounce on claims to its occurrence. Where allegations of miracle are concerned, science must be given a fair hearing; but it will be strangely forgetful of its own achievements and ambitions should it seek to rule out of court any alleged event as impossible, and even more strangely blind to its own limitations should it be tempted to overstep its rôle and become judge instead of advocate.

4

Preaching on the Resurrection

A DISADVANTAGE attendant on any pedantic adherence to the rhythm of the Christian Year is that it seems to confer on particular Sundays a monopoly of what belongs to every day, and so to obscure the timeless behind the occasional. When, for Dale of Birmingham, the doctrine of Christ's Resurrection itself arose from the dead, ceasing to be the cold marble of intellectual dogma and turning into flame, becoming a sun which brought life to his whole being, he instituted the practice of including a hymn of the Resurrection in every Sunday morning order of service. He had come to see that Easter Day is no single day in the calendar but the era in which the Church lives; and that the doctrine of the Resurrection is not just one among others, but the keystone of the sublime arch which rides from heaven to earth and earth to heaven, so that its subtraction would involve the collapse of the structure. You may not approve the method used to express these convictions, but you must surely sympathize with the motive behind it. For the New Testament rings with the Resurrection: indeed, it is hardly too much to say that the Evangel *is* the good news of the Resurrection.

Moreover, if you were to excise every reference to the Resurrection from the New Testament, you would have left on your hands a book not less but more puzzling than the book we have, for you would find events leading to results exactly opposite to what, by every consideration of moral probability and on every analogy drawn from our actual experience of life, they might be expected to lead. It simply wouldn't make sense. If you cut out the Resurrection as an impossibility, you are left with another impossibility. As the story is in fact told and continued—that is, with the narratives of the Resurrection as its determinative watershed—it remains, from one point of view, a baffling story: it doesn't make the kind of sense which our age is apt to acclaim as really good sense, namely, the kind of sense which you can demonstrate under laboratory conditions, and proceed to wield and apply practically, infallibly inducing situation 'B' from situation 'A' and doing it over and over again, to the presumed benefit of yourself and your fellows. The story doesn't fit that kind of pattern: the 'once for all' element in it forbids that. Talleyrand understood that well when, consulted by an advocate of a fancy new man-made religion who was disappointed with its progress, he asked, 'Could you not try being crucified, *and rising again from the dead?*' If you insist that the pattern of knowledge familiar in the laboratory is the sole pattern of real and useful knowledge, you will doubtless dismiss the story of the Resurrection as an irrelevance and an absurdity. But in another point of view, the biblical point of view, the story is like the sun, too blinding to be looked at directly but the source of the light by which you see everything else and of the warmth you live by. Ideally, from every occasion of Christian worship, whether hymns of the Resurrection have been sung or not, Christian people should carry the conviction, which their worship has afresh confirmed, that 'Christ being raised from the dead dieth no more; death hath no more dominion over him. For in that he died, he died unto sin once; but in that he liveth, he liveth unto God.' Stepping out from their churches, Christians step into a world to all appearance under the dominion of sin and death. How they comport themselves in it—whether carnally or cravenly, or with stoic endurance, or creatively in faith, hope and love—is going to depend on the measure in which this article of the faith has possessed them and illuminated the whole field of existence for them. How central the doctrine is we can judge from what St. Paul said when he contemplated the idea of a 'Christian' preaching with no Resurrection in it:

> 'Now if Christ is preached that he hath been raised from the dead, how say some among you that there is no resurrection of the dead? But if there is no resurrection of the dead, neither hath Christ been raised: and if Christ hath not been raised, then is our preaching vain, your faith also is vain. . . . For if the dead are not raised, neither hath Christ been raised: and if Christ hath not been raised, your faith is vain; ye are yet in your sins. Then they also which are fallen asleep in Christ have perished. If in this life only we have hoped in Christ, we are of all men most pitiable.' (I Cor. 15. 12–19.)

What has been said up to this point would probably command the assent of most Christians, provided the question is not raised of what exactly is meant by 'Resurrection'. All Christians are agreed that in some sense Jesus was victorious over death and lives for ever, the exalted Lord and Saviour of His people; but in the view of many this faith can be held without loss of substance independently of a belief in a corporal resurrection. The mode of our Lord's victory over death, they maintain, is a matter of minor importance about which we can afford to disagree. I propose to devote the major part of this lecture to examining this contention.

It may be well to begin by recalling in broad outline the main characteristics of different views that are held on this matter. First, there is the view of Catholic orthodoxy, of which Bishop Charles Gore may be taken as a typical British spokesman of modern times. He starts from a fact about which there is no dispute—the transformation of the disciples between the Crucifixion and their appearance in Jerusalem as fearless evangelists, and he notes that it was 'a corporate transformation which . . . suggests the impact of some startling fact of common experience'. He holds that this can be accounted for by nothing less than the historicity of the narratives of the empty tomb and appearances of the risen Lord. The fact of the empty tomb seems to him to be 'as indisputable as any fact of history'. He goes on to examine the evidence of St. Paul and contends that, although Paul nowhere mentions the empty tomb, he conceives of the Resurrection in a way which implies belief in it. In I Cor. 15, the apostle has in mind three different kinds of resurrection: that of Christ on the third day after death; that of since departed Christians, whose bodies have 'suffered corruption'; and the sudden transformation of those who shall be alive at the Second Coming.

> 'In all three classes of cases,' says Gore, 'St. Paul conceives a transformation more or less gradual or sudden of the natural body into the spiritual—"we shall all

be changed"—and quite plainly he finds the norm or pattern in the resurrection of Christ, in whose case he plainly conceives in the simplest manner that in respect of that body in which He died and *was buried*, in respect of that same body He was raised. . . . His condition was one of which hitherto men had never had experience. His spiritual body was material indeed, but it was one in which matter was wholly subservient to spiritual purpose, and no longer in any way an impediment or restraint.'[1]

The rest of the section is devoted to an attempt to harmonize the narratives of the post-resurrection appearances, and the conclusion is this:

'My contention is, then, that the historical evidence for the resurrection of our Lord the third day from the dead and His subsequent manifestations of Himself to His apostles is in the highest degree cogent. Nothing can resist it except that sort of treatment of the narratives which can render insecure almost any historical evidence.'[1]

The outstanding features of this typical view of Catholic orthodoxy would seem to be three.

(1) For the first believers the Resurrection of Christ was not an article of faith in the same sense in which it must be that for us, for it had been attested in immediate sense experience. It belonged to the same plane of reality as did the crucifixion of Jesus which men had seen with their eyes, and not to the same plane as does the being of God

[1] *The Reconstruction of Belief*, pp. 268–69.

the Father whom no man hath seen or can see. It was thus not something to which their faith rose, but something on which their faith was grounded.

(2) On the basis of the Resurrection fact the apostles were enabled to rise to the Resurrection faith, that cosmic faith which is Christianity, that faith in God which is epitomized in this classic New Testament description of Christian believers:

> '. . . you, Who by him (Christ) do believe in God, that raised him up from the dead, and gave him glory; that your faith and hope might be in God.' (I Pet. I. 21.)

The Resurrection not merely tolerated, but cogently thrust upon them, the interpretation of a supernatural deed of divine power in which, in response to that ultimate act and climax of faith whereby Jesus had given Himself to death for the world's sin, His total personality was brought back from the state of death and raised into a new mode of being which resumed in a transmuted form His corporal as well as His spiritual nature.

(3) Being a supernatural deed of God the Creator, the Resurrection cannot be rationalized in the narrower sense of being explained in terms of known and manipulable physical sequences. An inrush of omnipotent power shatters the test-tubes of science. But the very faith which perceives in the Resurrection a supernatural deed of divine power does so perceive it through recognizing its rationality in a larger sense—that is to say, its congruity, its necessity in that realm of reality which faith apprehends and within which, as Barth once put it, 'a question

mark is actually the ultimate fact of each of the sciences'.[1] In other words, though we cannot scan the mode of the Resurrection, we can apprehend its meaning: it was the springboard of the Church's faith in God's redeeming power, just as the manner of Christ's dying was the springboard of faith in His forgiving love. As Gore puts it:

> 'What the disciples needed and received in His corporal resurrection was the assurance that the power of God—the Creator and ruler of the whole world, material and moral—was, in spite of the seeming failure of the Cross, on the side of Jesus. In this supreme crisis nothing could reassure them but such an evidence of divine power undefeated—such a foretaste of the day of the Lord, the day when God is to come into His own. . . . It is only a corporal miracle such as the Resurrection of Jesus which gives us the needed reassurance that there is only one sovereignty in the universe, the sovereignty of the righteous God, the Father of our Lord Jesus Christ, and that in the full meaning of the term "Jesus is Lord." '[2]

[1] *The Word of God and the Word of Man*, p. 192. The passage runs: 'Every science knows well that there is a minus sign in front of its parenthesis; and the hushed voice with which that sign is ordinarily spoken of betrays the secret that it *is* the nail from which the whole science hangs; *it* is the question mark that must be added to the otherwise structurally perfect logic. If this question mark is really the ultimate fact of each of the sciences, it is evident that the so-called academic cosmos is an eddy of scattered leaves whirling over a bottomless pit. And a question mark *is* actually the ultimate fact of each of the sciences.'

[2] *Op. cit.*, p. 272.

On the left wing of Liberalism we find a view which, either explicitly or implicitly, denies all three positions just outlined.

(1) According to this view, the historical fact of Jesus—the fact directly attested within the sense experience of men—terminated with His death and burial. The life of Jesus and His death on the cross constitute the factual data on which Christianity was built. The Resurrection was a construct of faith, a conviction to which the first disciples rose—it was in their minds and spirits, and not in event outside them, that any miracle of corporal resurrection was wrought. The story of the empty tomb must be understood by us as 'holy saga', the medium in which their faith wrote itself down, like a rainbow printed by sunlight on April mists. If there were appearances of Christ after His death, these must be interpreted as 'holy hallucinations', neither owing their existence nor being rightly attributed to any impact of any exterior embodied reality upon the senses of those who experienced them. As instinct can conscript the machinery of the mind and rationalize a situation to its own satisfaction, so here a faith reached antecedently to the appearances conscripted the sensory machinery and created them. They were not a life-line thrown from heaven to the wreck of the apostles' hopes, but spider filaments produced within the organism of the primitive Church whereby it finally spun the web of catholic orthodoxy. Whatever their subjects thought of the appearances, we must interpret them as deposits of faith, not as data for it.

(2) Again, according to this view, the Resurrection may not be understood as a supernatural event which broke in upon nature in such wise that a dead body did

not suffer decay and dissolution, but rose in glory. I do not remember ever having seen it asserted that such an event could not possibly have happened—not even in the heyday of the rationalist attack on Christianity, and certainly not since the scientists have discovered the infinite plasticity of matter to spirit. The ground taken is generally rather that the evidence at our disposal is inadequate to warrant the belief. Here, for instance, is what one of Gore's critics wrote in an article in *The Hibbert Journal*, which as notably exemplified the Liberal view as Gore's book had the Catholic. The writer was examining the argument that 'we cannot account for the Apostles' enthusiasm apart from the belief that Jesus had been raised from the dead', and this is what he wrote:

> 'In default of this belief it is certainly difficult to account for the apparently sudden change from depression and despair to joyful faith. But to say that it *cannot* be accounted for on other grounds is to assume a knowledge of the relation between cause and effect in a given case which we do not possess. The faith of the Apostolic Church must be viewed, not from the point of view of presuppositions made *ex post facto* and with admittedly contradictory and meagre material to work upon, but from the point of view of human psychology *as a whole*, and in this region of inquiry the limits of the "possible" or "impossible" are beyond human computation. We are not affirming that other considerations must have entered into the apostolic faith (a faith that, we are told, can only be explained by the Resurrection) we are only saying that they *may*, and that the change in the outlook of the Apostles

may be legitimately viewed from the angle of this possibility.'[1]

Two things are evident from this passage.

(*a*) The writer would seem to hold that the change from despair to faith, even though it could not be explained except by a corporal resurrection, would be a much less uncomfortable mystery to have on hand than would be the mystery of a corporal resurrection. In other words, he would appear to hold that it is much easier to compute the limits of the possible or impossible in the realm of matter than in that of spirit; and, if there must be mystery, much prefers a psychological to a biophysical enigma.

(*b*) But the writer's attitude would seem to be determined, not by the evidence in the case nor the lack of it, but by other considerations which he brings to the study of it. Indeed, we have his express statement to this effect:

> 'We are not concerned to examine the evidence for the Resurrection, not only because it is no part of our immediate purpose, but because we are convinced that it is not on those grounds that this stupendous event will be admitted into the Christian system or denied a place in it. As Pascal says, "The soul has reasons of which the reason knows nothing," an axiom that can be applied as much to the negative as to the positive school of thought on this perplexing question.'

(3) When we enquire what are these 'reasons of the soul', we come upon a round denial of the third outstanding feature of Catholic orthodoxy:

[1] R. Rhynd, 'Bishop Gore on Miracles', *Hibbert Journal*, October, 1931.

> 'On the lofty level of thought on which the mind of Jesus worked, "miracle" appears as an alien element, and to insist on it as an essential ingredient in His moral authority as a teacher "sent from God" is to honour Him less than is generally imagined.'

And again:

> 'Some of the events recorded in the early chapters of the Acts are of such a kind as to strain our credulity to breaking-point, nor is it merely a question of credulity, but of congruity. The dignity and moral beauty of apostolic faith is not enhanced by these preposterous stories which drag it to the level of that pagan religion it was destined to replace.'

Instead of being accounted the fitting consummation of the story of Jesus, as being the Father's sovereign response to the faith of the Son, a corporal resurrection is thus held to be a barbarous anti-climax, the superlative instance of a crude and spurious supernaturalism such as enlightened faith must firmly reject.

For the purpose in hand it is unnecessary to indicate intermediate positions between the extremes of which examples have been given—like that, for instance, in which the story of the empty tomb is assessed as mythical but the stories of the appearances accepted as being based on experiences to be ranked as objective and non-hallucinatory. It is enough to have reminded you of the extreme positions for the purpose of showing that what is believed concerning the mode of the Resurrection is no matter of indifference. For the position taken by anyone on this matter will either show that he has already answered, or else determine how he must answer, at least three other vital questions, and cannot but affect profoundly the substance and tone of his preaching.

(1) First, there is the question of the extent to which, and the sense in which, we can trust the gospel records when they purport to deal with matters of fact. *Prima facie*, the Resurrection narratives are plain accounts of events of sense experience. Two questions at once emerge: were the apostles trustworthy witnesses regarding matters of fact? Does the New Testament faithfully preserve their original testimony?

I cannot see how we can answer the former of these questions in the negative without throwing a fatal cloud over the whole story of Jesus and, more than that, without incriminating any and every historical document. From the gospels themselves we get a convincing impression that the apostles were plain, common-sense men, the leading figures among them being extrovert in temperament and of the type which produces the most desirable witnesses in a court of law. Fishermen who have to earn their living by fishing are not easy to delude on points of fact, whatever amateur anglers may be like. Neither are revenue officials, nor a temperamental sceptic like Thomas.

If, then, we reject the stories of the Resurrection, it must be on the basis of a negative answer to the second question—if not roundly negative, at least negative in its effect upon the common-sense mind. Here is such an answer, carefully framed and beautifully expressed, which you will find in an important appendix to Otto's *The Idea of the Holy:*

> 'As regards the narratives of the "Empty Tomb", we shall judge of these as of the narratives of a later date

which gathered about the birth of Jesus, appraising them as a holy legend, in which the supra-rational relation of the eternal to temporal life is mirrored in the medium of contemporary thought. They have an enduring value to us from the incomparable beauty and power with which they symbolize the essence of the "mystery". We would not be without them in our Bible, nor yet in the pictorial art of the churches, nor in the hymns which express our devotion. And we can retain them thus without being false to the obligation of the most rigid honesty if we remain fully conscious of that other obligation, without fulfilling which we neither can nor should have either biblical instruction nor Christian doctrine. And that is the obligation we are under to train ourselves and the mind of our time to a sincere and devout understanding of three things.

In the first place, we need to realize the fringe of legend that surrounds the entire narrative of Holy Scripture and recurs as a constant problem from the first page of the Bible to the last.

Secondly, we need to appreciate the signal value and beauty and the profound import which distinguishes the biblical narrative even where it is of the nature of legend.

And finally, the fact that even in the holy saga and legend shaped and fashioned unconsciously by the spirit of a people or a fellowship, there is present the very same eternal Spirit of God, which Hebrew prophecy and poetry and history also manifest, that Spirit which, in every form of its expression, is the Spirit of revelation and truth.'[1]

[1] *The Idea of the Holy*, p. 235.

It is one thing to admit the general truth thus expressed that a fringe of legend surrounds the biblical narrative, and quite another to say that the fringe bites so deep into the garment that it includes the stories of the Resurrection. The problem is to discern where garment ends and fringe begins. And light will be thrown on that problem if we turn to another which comes to its sharpest focus on this same ground of the Resurrection narratives.

(2) On what kind of ultimate basis do our Christian beliefs rest? Let us again hear Otto on this question:

> ' "I *know* that my Redeemer liveth": "I *believe* in Jesus Christ, risen from the dead": such is the Christian's confession. "I know" and "I believe" or "have faith"—these are not here mutually exclusive expressions. This "knowing" is not that with which scientific theory is concerned, based upon empirical sense-knowledge; it is rather *faith-knowledge*, and faith-knowledge does not rely on the evidence of the senses, but is, in the scriptural phrase, "the evidence of things not seen", that is, not presented to sense-perception; and it would lose its essential nature and be transformed into a mere sorry empirical knowledge, if it relied on any other evidence than "the witness of the Holy Spirit", which is not that of sense-experience. And so we cannot afford to account Christ's resurrection, and our own, known facts, in this lower "scientific" sense of knowledge. The simplest understanding feels this. To speak of "resurrection" is to utter a mystery, and mystery is a subject for faith, not science. And, for Christianity, how this faith itself comes to be is no less a mystery, indeed the greatest of all mysteries. But if "faith" were knowledge, directly

attested by the senses or based upon a tradition of a former occurrence attested by the senses, this mystery would wholly disappear.'[1]

But, does what Otto calls 'mere sorry empirical knowledge' not necessarily enter somehow into the foundations of faith? How could there have been Christian faith without an empirical fact of Jesus of Nazareth? Are we to describe as 'mere sorry empirical knowledge' our assurance that Jesus lived, spoke the parables, exercised a ministry of healing, was crucified under Pontius Pilate? There questions answer themselves: such empirical facts are integral to Christianity, and if it be cut loose from them, it ceases to be Christianity and becomes a mere sorry speculative gnosticism. The real problem is not whether faith can afford to dispense with a basis of empirical fact, but rather what was the historical basis on which the Church's cosmic faith was built; and, further, whether it could have been built, and can be maintained, on a basis not including the fact of the Resurrection.

If the Resurrection be subtracted, one or other of two results must follow, as it seems to me. Either we must suppose that the apostles contrived to believe, and must ourselves contrive to believe, in God's victorious vindication of Jesus in the face of facts spelling defeat; or else we must drastically revise our ideas of victory and vindication. Either we must bring in a verdict in favour of a righteous cosmos against all the evidence, or else try the case again under new moral statutes.

On the former side of the alternative, we must believe in the righteous government of the world on no other

[1] *The Idea of the Holy*, p. 228.

evidence than that Jesus suffered in obedience and faith towards God and in forgiving love towards sinful men, and passed thus into the silence and power of death. But could these facts by themselves have evoked a cosmic faith in the hearts of the apostles of Jesus who had deserted Him at the last, and can they in ours? To suppose that they could or can creates a mystery not on a supra-rational but on a sub-rational level—not a mystery like that imaged in the sun, so bright that you cannot look into its burning heart but that it enables you to see everything else; rather a mystery of darkness blotting out all familiar roads. It is like supposing that you will make better sense of *Job* by going straight on from Chapter 37. 24 to Chapter 42. 10.

On the other side of the alternative we must hold that the Cross was not just a necessary prelude to the glory of the Son and the victory of the Father, but the actual substance of it. A. B. Davidson once commented on this idea in a characteristically dry way:

> 'It contains,' he wrote, 'a fine modern idea, but one to which Scripture has hardly yet advanced. The humiliation of the Son with his death is a "grace" (II Cor. 8. 9) and a proof of love (John 15. 13; Rom. 5. 8), but Scripture does not seem to have allowed itself the paradox of calling it a glory.'[1]

More satisfying is the less caustic and fuller statement of H. R. Mackintosh:

> 'The meaning of Christ was the disclosure of the Father as perfectly love, but it is frequently overlooked that this love could not be recognized as perfect save as

[1] Commentary on *Hebrews*, footnote, p. 59.

exhibited in prevailing absolute *power* as well as appealing moral beauty. Apart from the experience of an *almighty* love in the experience of the Revealer, the content of the revelation must have been fragmentary and ambiguous. Resurrection, therefore, crowned the demonstration of God's love as the absolute power to which all reality is subservient, and which no sin of man or independent ordinance of nature can ever defeat.'[1]

The Resurrection is thus the supreme instance of the infinite resourcefulness of God the Father. Its significance is not that Jesus of Nazareth survived death, but that the Christ of God *conquered* death and in principle abolished it; that in and through His own particular, historical dying on the Cross—that once-for-all act of dying in which the paradox of passion and action is brought into its acutest focus, in which He 'became sin' for mankind, subjected Himself freely in body, mind and spirit to all that sin means and entails, drew all that into His own breast like the Swiss knight who gathered the Austrian spears into his heart that a lane of victory might be made for his comrades, and offered Himself thus stricken to the Father—through *that* death, death was not merely survived but conquered. For, in response to that supreme uniting act of faith and love between God and man, God acted out of the infinite resources eternally at His command by reversing the law of sin and death and raising His Son from the grave as the first fruits of the new creation in Him.

(3) A third question is raised in its acutest form on this

[1] *The Person of Jesus Christ*, p. 372.

critical ground of the Resurrection, the question of the relation of 'matter' to 'spirit', and about it I shall make only a few simple remarks, the substance of which has been largely anticipated in what has already been said.

Those who reject a corporal resurrection would seem to hold one of the following positions or both: (*a*) we do not need, still less do we desire to have Christian faith, which is a 'spiritual' conviction, tied to manifestations in the 'material' realm; (*b*) knowing what we do of the matter-spirit relationship, we can be sure enough that a corporal resurrection did not happen.

(*a*) Here I would want simply to turn the tables on the writer earlier quoted, and say that on the lofty level of thought on which the Bible works, 'matter' and the miracles of which 'matter' may be vehicle and medium appear as integral elements, and to try to expunge them as unworthy ingredients in God's revelation of Himself is to honour Him less than is sometimes imagined. Well did the author of *Job* realize that: he saw that there can be no valid doctrine of redemption which is not firmly tied up with a doctrine of creation; Job's deliverance only comes when his moral and spiritual instincts are justified by a vision of a material universe created and controlled by God. And did not Jesus Himself once say, '. . . that ye may know that the Son of man hath power on earth to forgive sins . . . I say unto thee, Arise, take up thy bed, and go unto thine house'? But the ghost of the Manichaean heresy, which haunts the verandahs of Liberalism, is hard to lay.

(*b*) And do we really know enough about the spirit-matter relationship to be sure enough that a corporal resurrection did not happen? May it not be that we know next to nothing as yet about the potentialities of the mysterious spirit-matter union?

> 'This main miracle that I am I,
> With power in mine own act and on the world'

has been marvellously illustrated and enforced since Tennyson wrote the line—marvellously and menacingly. A little cloud no bigger than a man's hand has appeared above the human horizon. It would appear that the main miracle that man is man with power in his own act and on the world might conceivably bring about the end of the world in a limitless conflagration, so great may prove to be the power of man's spirit over matter and so little his restraint and reverence in the use of it. But, on the supposition of men being restored to their due communion with their Creator, there are other conceivable issues of the spirit-matter marriage. In one of his greatest casts of thought, St. Paul dwells on such possibilities:

> 'For the earnest expectation of the creature waiteth for the manifestation of the sons of God. . . . Because the creature itself also shall be delivered from the bondage of corruption into the glorious liberty of the children of God.'

The late Poet Laureate clearly had this passage in mind when he wrote:

> 'This world is unto God a work of art,
> Of which the unaccomplished heavenly plan
> Is hid in life within the creature's heart,
> And for perfection looketh unto man.'[1]

[1] Robert Bridges, *The Growth of Love*, stanza 16.

And perhaps it was in the background of his mind also when he elsewhere wrote these lovely lines, which enshrine the inmost thought of St. Paul, although they lack his passionate yearning:

> 'And if some beauteous things—whose heavenly worth
> And function overpass our mortal sense—
> Lie waste and unregarded on the earth
> By reason of our gross intelligence,
> These are not vain, because in nature's scheme
> It lives that we shall grow from dream to dream
> In time to gather an enchantment thence.'[1]

In the faith of the Church, which is nothing at all if not a cosmic faith, the Resurrection of Christ is at once the pledge and the dynamic of this consummation.

This lecture has hardly justified its title: I must apologize for having been so apologetical, instead of observing the proper limits of homiletics. Let me at least make a courtesy bow to the title in two concluding practical counsels.

Let your preaching ring with Resurrection, as did the Apostles', and that not only on Easter morning, but whenever you seek to counter sin and despair and death in the human heart. Preach it to men who have sinned in the flesh and know the sting of the body's degradation, that they may have faith in Him who, having become sin for them and felt in His crucified body the pangs of sin's punishment, rose in a glorious body of God's fashioning and in that body devotes Himself to their salvation—body, mind and spirit. Preach it fearlessly to men of

[1] Robert Bridges, *Eros and Psyche*, April, stanza 6.

learning and science: there is a Christian assurance of a new heaven and a new earth which far outshines the brave new world of applied science, without for one moment disowning its humanitarian zeal. Preach it to the bereaved. Preach it to all sorts and conditions of men.

But always as you preach it, remember so to preach it that you do not obscure this inmost paradox of Christianity: faith in Him who raised up Jesus from the dead and gave Him glory gives us victory and life; but the victory and life it gives for our mortal days is the power to die daily in the image of Christ's death, that at the last we may be found alive in Him—that so may come

> 'the miracle,
> The marriage feast of Heaven and Earth,
> Of which on earth we cannot tell
> Save in such words: a Death, a Birth.'[1]

As in the ancient world all roads led to Rome, so all the roads of Christian doctrine lead into eschatology.

[1] Edwin Muir, *The Year's Christmas*, the poem already quoted from.

5

Preaching on the Last Things

LET US START from two sayings which in different ways convey the same admonitory hint to preachers. The first was spoken long ago in a New College class-lecture by that rugged, shrewd and fundamentally sweet-natured scholar, Professor Adam Welch. 'The two chief faults of ministers,' he said, 'are downright laziness and the habit of saying just a little more than they have any personal right to say.' The other was uttered in private conversation by Dr. George Shaw Stewart of Gorgie, a minister of Christ who alluringly and disturbingly mirrored his Master. We had been talking about preaching and the different ways one comes at subjects for the approaching Sunday. I had said what a relief it was when a good text occurred to you, especially if you had been gravelled for one and were beginning to worry. And then, neither priggishly nor magisterially, but as though he were making a trite remark about the weather, he said that he made it a rule never to preach from a text which he hadn't tried to live by for six months. A man of his quality does not mean to be shattering, but he shatters you all the same, just by being himself.

Both these sayings raise the question whether there may be things besides visions and revelations of the Lord which it is not lawful for a man to utter, and reasons for reticence less creditable to him than that he has been caught up to the third heaven. In his essay on Character, Emerson says that in nature all things work exactly according to their quantity and quality—all except man. 'But man has pretension, wishing and attempting things beyond his force.' He recalls how an eighteenth-century British statesman, when a government was being formed, insisted on having the Treasury and nothing short of it, because, as he claimed, 'he had served up to it', and contrasts with him 'a certain amiable and accomplished person who undertook a practical reform'. 'But,' Emerson goes on, 'I was never able to find in him the enterprise of love he undertook. He adopted it by ear and by the understanding from the books he had been reading. All his action was tentative, a piece of the city carried out into the fields, and was the city still, and no new fact, and could not inspire enthusiasm.' Hence the conclusion: 'We shall still postpone our existence, nor take the ground to which we are entitled, whilst it is only a thought, and not a spirit, that incites us. We have not yet served up to it.'

Does this apply to preaching? Are there texts and themes and ranges of the Christian truth which, even when we possess them in our minds and understanding from the books we have been reading and the lectures we have been hearing, we had far better avoid until 'we have served up to them'? Is 'pulpit pretension' one of the reasons why the immeasurable flood of Christian utterance which deluges the world—millions upon millions of goodly words poured out daily, and reaching astronomical figures on Sundays—should be so little fructifying, as we sometimes despondingly feel?

It is easier to raise such questions than to give round answers to them, but some aspects of the matter are plain enough. Authentic personal experience gives to any utterance on any subject a power of assault and a skill of entry derivable from no other source; and this applies in a special way to the realm of religion, the subject-matter of which is precisely the truth of personal existence. Very quickly, as you listen to a preacher, you begin to sense whether his words are the flowering of a life or just the frothing of a mind; whether he is a genuine traveller or only a clerk in the office of Thomas Cook & Son. You feel this whether or not he is a good preacher in a superficial sense. He may be an expert technician, one of those 'workmen good' who 'reach to their end by steps well understood'; he may even be the artist in whom dwells 'an instinct throned in reason's place'; and all that will be gain and grace, like a well-cut suit of clothes.[1] But all that does not add up to integrity, and may only produce felicitous emptiness. Walford Davies, adjudicating at a musical festival once shook a complacent church choir by denying to it the award on which it had counted and adding, as they thought, insult to injury in the comment that their burnished performance had reminded him of a beautiful corpse. I have heard sermons like that and, on the other hand, at least two which scandalously broke all the approved rules of sermon-making and were none the-less unforgettably powerful. One was on the text, 'Harden not your hearts', and was preached by an undistinguished-looking middle-aged little man taking a day's pulpit supply at a holiday resort. He spoke, like Paul at Corinth,

[1] See the opening stanzas of Robert Bridges' *The Growth of Love*, where the contrast is beautifully presented.

'in weakness and fear and much trembling'; he lost all control of grammar and syntax; he made uncouth gestures; he writhed about in a distressed manner as though in physical pain. But the hallmark of integrity was stamped on the confusions and contortions, so that the tragedy of the heart hardened against God by lust or worldliness or pride, of which the preacher spoke as though he were the reluctant reporter of obscenities, was brought powerfully home that morning. 'Not with enticing words of man's wisdom, but in demonstration of the Spirit and of power.' The other such sermon was one preached by Dr. James Graham of Kalimpong on the text, 'God is love.' There can rarely have been delivered in a university chapel a discourse structurally more ramshackle or spiritually more impressive. In his later years Dr. Graham brought to the pulpit an asset which cannot be bought cheap or stolen or counterfeited, but only 'served up to'— a face engraved with the love and sorrow of a life long dedicated to Christ. One of his hearers out in India once described it as 'a love-letter to the human race'. Whenever that morning he repeated his text, and he did so many times, his face lit up from within in an undescribable way; and it is hardly too much to say that thereby the whole Gospel was instantaneously preached.

Now, the moral of all this is not for one moment that you and I can afford to dispense with the well-tried techniques of the preacher's art, and still less that we should conscientiously cultivate pulpit contortions or keep anxiously looking into mirrors to see how our faces are coming along. On the contrary, we must earnestly strive all our lives to master the techniques, but to remember all the while how empty is artistry without integrity, and how nowhere is it truer than in preaching that 'the gift without the giver is bare'.

But what has just been said needs to be supplemented from another angle. At conferences or other gatherings of ministers, when I have quoted the sayings from which we started and spoken on the lines we have been following, invariably in subsequent discussion a contribution has been made to the following effect: 'That is all very well up to a point; but if it were to be accepted without qualification, we should never open our mouths in the pulpit at all. Doubtless integrity is essential to preaching; but integrity does not mean moral perfection, or a life in which dream and deed are one, or even a complete intellectual grasp of Christian truth: it only means honest desire for these things and persevering effort after them. Moreover, the preacher, of whom as a person integrity may rightly be demanded, is also an official of the Church, a functionary of whom professional adequacy may rightly be expected, and not least adequacy in expounding the doctrines of the Church. To a good part of preaching the character of the preacher is more or less irrelevant: it is his intellectual grasp of the subject which really matters.'

There is substance in both these contentions. The paradox of the pulpit is that its occupant is a sinner whose chief right to be there is his perpetual sense that he has no right to be there, and is there only by grace and always under a spotlight of divine judgment. And certainly the pulpit ought to be the voice of the teaching Church, the place where 'all the counsel of God' is declared, as it has been made known to the Church and verified in its life down the centuries, and not merely the place where some bright young lad or some pompous old boy is obliging enough to give his personal certificate to certain aspects of Christian truth. Moreover, in proportion as a minister recognizes that he is under a professional obligation to deal with all the themes of the Church's faith and honestly seeks to discharge it, he is in fact helped to outgrow limitations which might otherwise render his pulpit ministry meagre and stunted. There are the limitations of the natural bent of mind and personality. In our apprehension of the faith we all begin at this or that point: a particular facet of the many-splendoured thing becomes incandescent for us since it corresponds to our individual disposition and need. Naturally, to begin with, that will be our most congenial topic, for about that we shall be able to speak with the greatest conviction; but the danger is that we may not explore and appropriate beyond it and may finally develop into pulpit-bores, saying much too little much too often at much too great length. The due recognition that ministers are ordained to be voices of the teaching Church will act as a stimulus to growth, inciting them to reach out towards a richer and deeper understanding of the faith of which they have been made official custodians; and this is a process in which there need be no loss of integrity so long as it engages the whole personality and not the mind only. The besetting sin of intellectuals is to bite off more than they choose.[1] By the same token, a man is helped to outgrow the limitations of

[1] Masefield's lines:

> 'But trained men's minds are spread so thin
> They let all kinds of darkness in;
> Whatever light man finds they doubt it,
> They love not light, but talk about it,'

might well be engraved as a warning above the portals of all theological seminaries.

theological fads and fashions, and to be eclectic rather than partisan in respect of them. Most important of all, if, looking towards the end of his ministry from the beginning of it, he cherishes the ambition to be able to say then what Paul said to the Ephesian elders at Miletus—that he had not shunned to declare to them all the counsel of God—he will be fortified against the insidious temptation always to be cashing in on popular moods and movements of the hour instead of speaking the Word that abideth for ever.

Integrity, artistry, adequacy—if a pulpit ministry grows continuously in these qualities, it may earn in the end the kind of judgment which Robert Lind passes on Dr. Johnson: 'he lifted a life of words to the level of a life of action.'

The preceding remarks have been introduced so far in their own right, but also to provide a background for what I have to say about preaching on the Last Things.

You will not have been long in your first pastoral charge before you will be called on to attend the sick, conduct funerals and visit in bereaved homes, sometimes in circumstances of great poignancy. Most young ministers find these duties trying, and would be abnormally saintly or abnormally shallow if they didn't. They feel embarrassed and inadequate in the performance of them, even while they say and read 'the right things' and otherwise comport themselves with professional propriety. The cause of the trouble isn't far to seek: it is that in respect of the Last Things—the whole realm of which any particular event or omen of death is monitor and memento—we all tend to live much deeper in oblivion or incredulity of the Church's faith than we do in respect of other elements and moments of it. You would think, would you not, that in the presence of death you could reckon on finding between Christian man and pagan man, and between Christian home and pagan home, a contrast as great as you find between the first chapter of I Peter, let us say, and the third chapter of Ecclesiastes or the forty-first chapter of Ecclesiasticus. But in fact the difference between the lives isn't nearly so striking as the difference between the literatures. In fact the working creed of too many of us Christians—our operative creed, the creed which makes the difference to the feel of the morning to ourselves and the look of our lives to others—is often far less like the doxology, 'Blessed be the God and Father of our Lord Jesus Christ, which, according to his abundant mercy, hath begotten us again unto a life of hope through the resurrection of Jesus Christ from the dead . . .' than like the sombre conclusion of Ecclesiastes:

> 'that which befalleth the sons of men befalleth beasts; even one thing befalleth them: as the one dieth, so dieth the other; yea, they have all one breath; so that a man hath no pre-eminence above a beast: for all is vanity';

or this from Ecclesiasticus:

> 'O death, how bitter is the remembrance of thee to a man that liveth at rest in his possessions, unto the man that hath nothing to vex him, and that hath prosperity in all things: yes, unto him that is yet able to receive meat! O Death, acceptable is thy sentence unto the needy, and unto him whose strength faileth, that is now in the last age, and is vexed with all things, and to him that despaireth, and hath lost patience!'

When men's working creed is of this latter sort, they naturally seek to push the thought of death away from them as far as they can, even though death is an omnipresent and obtrusive reality. Nicholas Berdyaev speaks of the 'insensitiveness to death and forgetfulness of it which are so characteristic of nineteenth and twentieth century ethics'. He says:

> 'The last achievement of the herd-mind is to try to forget about death altogether, to conceal it, to bury the dead as unobtrusively as possible. It is the very opposite of the spirit expressed in the Christian prayer "ever to remember death". In this respect modern civilized people are incomparably inferior to the ancient Egyptians.'[1]

But it is not markedly characteristic of Scottish churchmanship in our generation to pray 'ever to remember death', in which respect we differ much from the Christians of some past generations. Certainly the first generation of the faithful were taught and exhorted to hold together in a fruitful interplay two emphases—a this-worldly and an other-worldly: they were taught both to 'live soberly, righteously and godly in this present world', and to 'look for a blessed hope' beyond it; and they did either of these things with the greater fervour because they did the other. Whatever else they may be accused of, the Middle Ages cannot be accused of forgetting the Last Things. The first sentence of a historical work I have lost all trace of—I must have lent it to a brother minister—was this, 'The mediæval cathedrals were built on the fear of hell.' Throughout John Donne's sermons there runs a con-

[1] *The Destiny of Man*, p. 321.

tinuous *memento mori;* and of the congregations which thronged to hear him preach it has been said that 'the unthinkableness of eternity hag-rode their imaginations.' Churchyard inscriptions as late as the beginning of Victorianism witness to the solemn and pointed fashion in which the brevity of life and the certainty of death and the possibilities beyond death were held up before the eyes of these times.

In contrast to all this, we belong to an emphatically this-worldly generation of churchmanship, and part of the reason of it is not discreditable, being a reaction against very dubious ingredients in certain kinds of other-worldliness. For instance, we have seen that there must be something farcical and fraudulent in the kind of pietism which preaches from villas in the West End to slums in the East End about mansions in heaven. We have seen that certain kinds of 'materialism' are deeply 'spiritual' activities. We have awakened to the meaning of love of the brother in new ranges and reaches of relationship. We have become aware of the claims of social justice, not merely in the realm of immediate person-to-person contacts—master to servant, landlord to tenant, rich man to beggar, and so forth—but also as these ought to affect the structure of society and the distribution of the world's wealth, and as they are occasioning vast stirrings of ambition, resentment and passion among the under-privileged all over the world. We can honestly say with Oliver Cromwell, 'If any whosoever think the interests of Christians and the interest of the nation inconsistent, I wish my soul may never enter their secrets'; and we can say with John Wesley, although in a different sense from his, 'The world is our parish.' It is far from discreditable to contemporary churchmanship that it should display concerns and apprehensions of this kind. And yet nothing to plume ourselves upon, when you come to think of it: we should be fools as well as knaves if we failed to display them. Besides, it has taken Marx and the Communists to waken us afresh to these essential aspects of Christianity, and even under their grim tutorship our eyes are not fully opened to them yet. At any rate, it is difficult to believe that any robust Christian preacher will fail today to make room in his pulpit plans and programmes for the handling of social and political issues in which the honour of Christ and His Church is involved. And that urgent duty is made easier even for the timid in that there is flowing in the Church a strong current of concern about its this-worldly task, and because it is so clear that from a church which has nothing to say about such matters not much need be expected when it speaks about things less obvious.

In this situation three things need to be remembered:

(1) The nature of the Church on earth, the Pilgrim Church, is not well symbolized by a circle centred on a single focus: a truer symbolic diagram is an ellipse centred on two foci—the secular and the eternal, the mundane and the mystical—which are not the centres of separate circles, but twin determinants of the Church's witness and task. Treat them as separables and as retaining significance in divorce the one from the other, and you will surely land in your preaching either into that kind of sentimental pietism against which Communism is the mighty and just modern protest, or else into the kind of secular utopianism which is, as we in the Church believe, the mirage in the desert of contemporary life and thought. If the Church's message were to degenerate in the former way, then the

Church would as thoroughly deserve to be subjected to a communist tyranny as Jerusalem deserved to be subjected to Nebuchadnezzar. And you don't hold up the march of a Nebuchadnezzar by holding more and more services of worship—by merely chanting with more and more fervour, 'God's in His temple! God's in His very own temple!'—any more than you do by merely shouting uproariously, 'There'll always be a Jerusalem!' But if, on the other hand, the Church has nothing but a this-worldly message, even it be an urgent call to social justice, then it becomes what von Hügel somewhere calls 'an irritating superfluity, a feeble ditto to the State.' To keep the rhythm of the Church's witness true, both accents need to be maintained in their just interplay, and if you are to exercise an adequate pulpit ministry you must learn to strike both firmly and fairly, and not only one at the expense or to the eclipse of the other. To fail in either is to vitiate both.

(2) Broadly speaking, I venture to prophesy this: unless you take the proper measures to safeguard yourselves, you will tend to under-accent the other-worldly element in the Church's witness, and that in spite of the new prominence being given to it by the leaders of the Ecumenical Movement. It takes a long, long time for a lead given in Geneva to percolate to Auchtermuchty or Acharacle. Meanwhile, the hope of heaven is not a popular emphasis: it doesn't lie to the general mind and mood of our age; it's not scientific! It's an emphasis, moreover, which we are inclined to soft-pedal in proportion as the Marxian gibe about religion being the opiate of the people has stung us—its sting being, of course, the element of truth it may have in certain applications. Above all, it's an

emphasis which the natural man in you and me—the pagan man fighting for his life, the old Adam in principle dead, drowned in the waters of baptism, crucified with Christ, but in practice an expert in resurrection—resents and resists and will abandon on any excuse, especially a plausible excuse like the one just indicated. 'It is true,' whispers the old Adam in dulcet tones, 'that the fires of hell and the bliss of Paradise, where

> The gardens and the gallant walks
> Continually are green,
> Where grow such sweet and pleasant flowers
> As nowhere else are seen,
>
> And where they live in such delight
> Such pleasure and such play,
> As that to them a thousand years
> Doth seem as yesterday,

have been exploited and abused in the name of high religion—dangled before the economic beasts of burden to keep them moving. You must avoid that parody of religion at all costs, avoid even the appearance of that evil; and the surest way of doing that is to be silent about the Last Things altogether.' And you may not perceive that your real reason for giving ear to such a counsel is that on which the writer to the Hebrews lays an unerring finger, when he describes the partakers of flesh and blood as those 'who through fear of death were all their lifetime subject to bondage.' Our own lack of adjustment to death, our own feebleness of grasp of the faith which envisages an end—the end of our lives in the body, the end of the world, the end of history—these may be the real reasons which hide behind the plausible reasons and make us so eager to preach about housing on earth rather than about the mansions above.

To my mind, the most remarkable passage in that most remarkable book, *The Kon-Tiki Expedition*, is not any that describes the denizens of the deep or the adventures of the six splendid explorers, but one which tells us something about their feelings. Listen to this:

> 'It was most remarkable what a psychological effect the shaky bamboo cabin had on our minds. It measured eight by fourteen feet, and to diminish the pressure of wind and sea it was built so low that we could not stand upright under the ridge of the roof . . . and despite the fact that the bamboo wall on the starboard side was open for one third of its length, and roof and walls let in sun and moon, this primitive lair gave a greater feeling of security than white-painted bulkheads and closed portholes would have given in the same circumstances. . . . So long as we only kept on board, the bamboo hut and its jungle scent were plain reality and the tossing seas seemed rather visionary. . . . The longer the voyage lasted the safer we felt in our cosy lair, and we looked at the white-crested waves that danced past outside our doorway as if they were an unimpressive cinema show conveying no menace to us at all. Even though the gaping wall was only five feet from the unprotected edge of the raft and only a foot and a half above the waterline, yet we felt as if we had travelled many miles away from the sea and occupied a jungle dwelling remote from the sea's perils. There we could lie on our backs and look up at the curious roof which

twisted about like boughs in the wind, and enjoy the jungle smell of raw wood, bamboos and withered palm leaves.'[1]

Five feet from the edge of a raft in mid-Pacific and a foot and a half above the waterline, the infinities of sea and sky above and around, and beneath the water's glittering surface its unfathomable mystery and menace—and yet they felt remote from the sea's perils once they had crawled inside their crazy little bamboo cabin! What a story! And what a symbol of lives lived in these so vulnerable bodies of ours on this speck of a spinning planet, except that for many there is no faith such as buoyed up the six high-hearted Scandinavians of a landfall in the west!

A fact may suitably be interjected here which is worth pondering. At the Cambridge Conference on Evangelism held under the auspices of the British Council of Churches towards the end of the war, the then Director of Religious Broadcasting, Prebendary James Welch, told us that up to that date, out of all the war sermons preached on the British broadcasting system, not one had been offered by any preacher of any denomination on the subject of immortality.

(3) Nowhere will lack of integrity—saying 'the right things' perfunctorily, saying a little more than you have any personal right to say, especially saying loudly that little more—be more damaging in its effect than in respect of the Last Things.

But how can you 'serve up to' preaching about them? In the nature of the case, you cannot do so through direct

[1] Pp. 131–32.

experience, as you can in relation, let us say, to the doctrine of forgiveness. Neither will you necessarily do so by the simple process of growing older. William Ernest Hocking gives this analysis:

> 'We must note that the belief in one's own death is an acquired and usually a late belief, not at all a native one. The immediate feeling of life touches no limit either of beginning or end: to be alive is to expect that each next moment will be followed by another. . . . Neither terminus of life can be experienced; and neither can be realized in imagination. Hence the belief which every mature man acquires that his own death will come, is an intellectual adoption, not an intuitive faith.'[1]

But you do not necessarily become *mature* merely by growing older: I remember once reading in a novel about a character in whose case 'a prolonged adolescence merged in his early fifties with a premature senility'. And Axel Munthe, a man who reflected as much upon death as Hocking, if not so profoundly, makes this comment:

> '. . . the further we advance towards our graves, the further does Death recede from us. . . . Old people seldom talk about death, their dim eyes seem unwilling to focus anything but the past and the present. Gradually, as their memory weakens, even the past becomes more and more indistinct, and they live almost entirely in the present.'[2]

However these things may be, integrity in preaching on the Last Things requires that the preacher be striving to fulfil three conditions, whether he be young or old.

[1] *Thoughts on Death and Life*, pp. 17–18.

[2] *The Story of San Michele*, p. 504.

First, through the appropriate Christian disciplines of meditation and prayer, he must be seeking to grow into the realization that mortal life must always be fatally *shadowed* unless it is lived *sub specie æternitatis*. In the chapter just quoted from, Munthe thus apostrophizes the sun:

> 'God of day, Giver of light, cannot You stay with me a little longer? The night is so long for thoughts that dare not dream of sunrise, the night is so dark for eyes that cannot see the stars. Cannot you grant me a few seconds more of your radiant eternity to behold your beautiful world, the beloved sea, the wandering clouds, the glorious mountains, the rustling streams, the friendly trees, the flowers among the grass, the birds and beasts, my brothers and sisters, in the sky and in the forests and the fields? . . . Dear old nurse, who has dispelled so many evil thoughts from my burning forehead by the gentle stroke of your wrinkled old hand, do not leave me alone in the dark. I am afraid of the dark! Stay with me a little longer, tell me a few more of your wonderful fairy-tales while you put your restless child to bed for the long night's sleep.'

Which of us has not some time known that mood, and experienced the sense that time is our enemy? And so it is, most truly and bitterly our enemy, unless and until we can believe that every offering made to God in Time is accepted and treasured by the Eternal One, and will be received again by His servants in His consummated purpose. Contrast with Munthe's sad apostrophe utterances from a very different source, a sermon on Eternity preached long ago by a missionary of the Society of St. John the Evangelist:

'The man of the world looks for results which are all within this world, within his own little time and place in it. The man of faith looks beyond this world, while making the very best use of his time within it, and feels in regard to all that he does, "It is for eternity, because it is for God: these words, thoughts, acts—they do not perish as they pass from me; I sow them; we shall reap if we faint not." Eternity is not his *dream;* it is his very substance, it is himself, moving forward to the full result of the Divine purpose and call. . . . Generous souls scorn a life which is organized throughout on the basis of death; "you have but a minute to live: get what good you can out of it before you die". They feel that the mind of man is able to grasp eternity within the narrow space of the moment, and they claim eternity as their native sphere. . . . Thus all created things change and pass, but they do not come and go for nothing. We discover that every frailest creature, every little wild flower on the veld has a certain link with that which abides—with the eternal Love of God. You see a new spring come, and you watch it fade away with all its wealth, and yet it has left one treasure behind with you. Something in it of inexpressible refinement, of incomparable purity of colour, or delicacy of form has revealed to you that it is not a thing thrown off by accident in a mechanical process, but a clear utterance of the eternal Mind, of the eternal Love. As it passed away it left with you a word of God which is to contribute to your habitual desire of God—your abiding union with God—a joy which began with your delight in a wild plant, and ended with your delight in and praise of God. . . . The spiritual man will learn by the lightest touch of pure sensation, by the most evanescent impression of a moment, received from nature, or art, to be passing with delight or desire or praise to that which is eternal.'[1]

Secondly, and through the same disciplines of the Christian way of life, the preacher must be learning in mind and heart that our mortal life must always be in danger of being morally *shallow* unless it is lived in prospect of a final judgment at the bar of an absolute righteousness. This does not merely mean learning to live in the light of Christian principle, but preparing to meet a personal judge. A principle is an abstraction which *you* apply, and which leaves *you* in a sense master of the situation; a person is one whom you confront, whose will is not your will, whose judgment is not in your power. It is one thing to play chess against yourself—in that pastime you can make black or white win according as you please, and the record of the game will look all right, and yet be entirely phoney; it is quite another thing to face a personal opponent across the board who never abates the rigour of the game. So it is one thing to strive to live by Christian principle, and another to expect to stand before the judgment-seat of Christ, and to receive the things done in the body.

And, finally, the preacher must be learning that the life on earth, despite all its widths and depths of interest, is too *small* to satisfy the spirit which God has breathed into man.

I have never ventured to preach on one of the greatest texts of Scripture, its flight is too high. Paul has been rebuking the Corinthians for their divisions, who are

[1] George Congreve, *The Spiritual Order*, pp. 261–74.

priding themselves on being Pauline Christians, and Petrine Christians, and Apolline Christians, and what not —much like the underside of the Ecumenical Movement. He has been trying to argue and cajole and shame them out of it, because partisanship always ultimately means meagreness. And then, you remember, as though his spirit had tired of argument and rebuke and cajolery, or as though a vision had opened before him which made these procedures look paltry, he suddenly soars like an eagle in the empyrean words:

> 'For all things are yours; whether Paul, or Apollos, or Cephas, or the world, or life, or death, or things present, or things to come; all are yours; and ye are Christ's; and Christ is God's.

Such is the width of the Gospel we are commissioned to preach, a Gospel for time and for eternity. We shall never do more than stammer about it; but God can make the stammerings of small men, if they be humble and faithful, no less than the wrath of the proud, great dictators of earth though he may have permitted them to be, to redound to His praise and glory.